ADOBE ILLUSTRATOR MASTER GUIDE 2024

From Beginner to Pro | Exploring the Endless Possibilities with Adobe Illustrator

WisdomBytes Solutions

TABLE OF CONTENTS

INTRODUCTION

A lot of people use Adobe Illustrator to make and change digital pictures with smooth lines and curves, which are also called vector drawings. This book is helpful because it shows you how to use the newest version of this software. It is meant to help both new and experienced users get better at drawing and designing. The detailed guide "Adobe Illustrator 2024" goes over all of the features of the newest version of Adobe Illustrator. The book is written for people who want to become experts in graphic design and learn how to use Adobe software. This makes it easy for everyone to learn how to use this complex tool.

CHAPTER 1

WHAT'S NEW IN ADOBE ILLUSTRATOR 2024

In this introduction chapter, we will show you all of the new features that were just included in the Adobe Illustrator 2024 update and walk you through how to use them.

Text to Vector Graphic

First, we have the highly anticipated Text to Vector Graphics. To open this, go up to "Window" and select "Text to Vector Graphics."

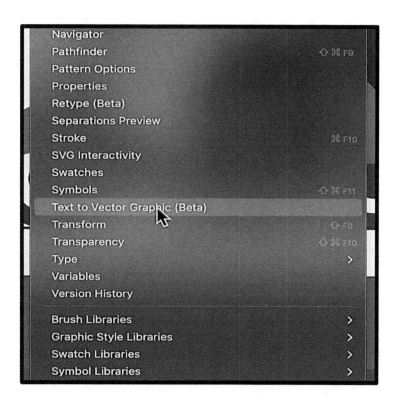

You can then use the shape tool to mark out the area where you want your graphic to be. In the right-hand panel, you can choose the type of graphic you want and use the eyedropper to sample the graphic style you desire.

If you submit your illustration here, it will attempt to match its style. Then simply write in what you want to make, select "Generate," and you'll be presented with a few possibilities. As you can see, this is a full vector graphic that can be scaled and moved about. Let us try to make a background scene for an image. We will sketch our shape on the artboard and send it to the rear. Then alter the type to be viewed, and we'll type our text, which for this example will be "airport." Do not forget to sample your photograph. After we've done that, we'll click "Generate," which will display a few results. As you can see, they aren't ideal, but they're a good start and certainly useful for quickly testing a notion. It does a good job of producing crisp vector artwork.

Retype tool

Next, we have the new Retype tool, which can recognize fonts in a picture and convert them into live text. To do so, select your image and then click "Type" and "Retype."

This will subsequently evaluate and highlight specific text regions in your image. Select the area you wish to identify, and it will show you a list of typefaces that fit it. You can sort these fonts by web fonts or system fonts.

If you find a typeface that you like, you can download it directly from Adobe by clicking the cloud symbol here. Once downloaded, **double-click the text on your image** to turn it into live text. Then, if you click **"Exit,"** you may type directly onto the image and move it wherever you like. This will be ideal for modifying graphics and prototyping designs.

Share for Review

The recently released Share for Review tool, which allows for seamless collaboration and client feedback, comes next. You can even share with people who do not have Creative Cloud accounts. To do this, simply select the **"Share" button** in the right-hand corner, enter your file name, set access, and click "**Create Link."**

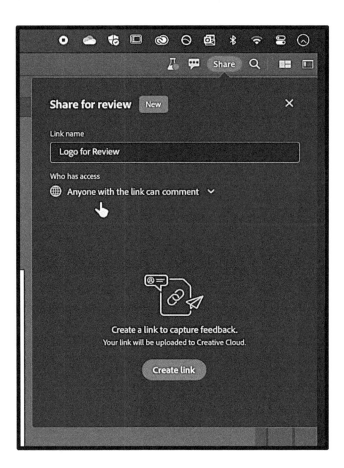

You may alter access settings and even add a password in the Share for Review window by choosing **"More Options" and then "Link Settings**." Hit the toggle here to establish your password. To ensure they're viewing the most recent designs, click "Update Content," then copy the URL to share.

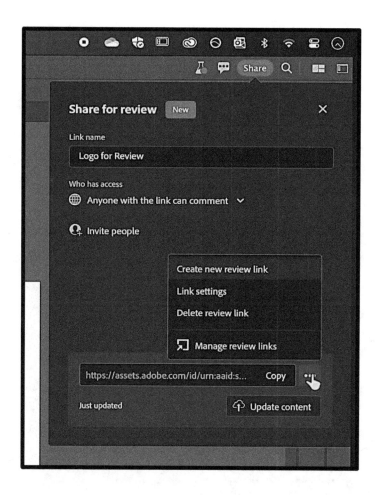

Recipients of the link can access it using the password you created. Then they can give any feedback on the design. They can even use pins to comment on specific sections or use the pen tool to point out changes and attach comments to them. All comments are live in your design file, allowing you to respond and make any necessary changes. If you don't see the comments window, click **"Window" and then "Comments."**

Whenever a change has been made, you can change the comment by clicking the message symbol here, which allows you to keep track of the changes you've made. Live comments can be turned on and off by clicking the Live symbol at the bottom, and you can also filter responses by reviewer, time, status, and unread comments. Once you've completed making changes, return to "**Share" and select "Update Content.**" This wonderful new tool will save you time and expedite the evaluation process.

The New Contextual Taskbar

Next, we have the new contextual taskbar, which displays the most important actions in your workflow. For example, if you choose a grouped object, it will display options such as recolor, ungroup, repeat object, duplicate object, and lock. When you pick text, you can alter the font, font size, area type, and outline it.

This bar might get a little bit annoying as it follows you around, so you can simply move it out of the way, and it's going to lock to the new position. To reset this, select "More Options" and go to "Reset bar position."

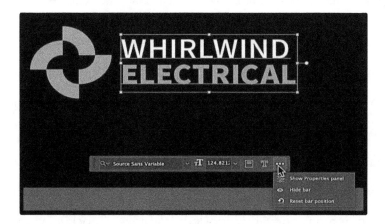

You can also hide the bar, which is going to remove it. To bring the contextual taskbar back, simply go up to "Window" and select "Contextual Taskbar."

The New Mockup Tool

Next, we have the new mockup tool, enabling you to apply your designs to any image. You may even try out the new Mockup library, which enables you to mock up your designs with just one click. First, locate an image of your mockup. Put your image into Illustrator, and then add your artwork. For example, suppose you wish to employ a vector-based logo. You can place it basically where you like in your image. Then, pick both the image and the artwork, and then choose **"Object," "Mockup," and "Make" from the menu.**

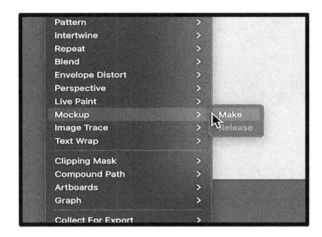

You can now drag your logo around the file to find the ideal spot for it. As you can see, it recognizes the geometry of your mockup and distorts your artwork accordingly. You can experiment with your blend modes under "Transparency" to achieve a more realistic effect. If you have an Adobe Stock account, you can also choose from a library of pre-designed mockup templates for a variety of projects, ranging from branding visuals to digital devices, which will save you a lot of time when preparing client presentations. To achieve this, activate the mockup window by choosing "Window," "Mockup" from your top menu. Now, with your artwork selected, select the mockup button. This will apply the artwork to all of the mockup templates. Choose "Edit on Canvas," then double-click your design to modify the frame.

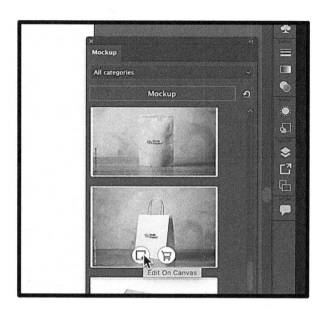

The Smooth Tool

Last but not least, the Smooth Tool. To demonstrate this, let's draw a wobbly line. With your line selected, navigate to "Object," "Path," and "Smooth."

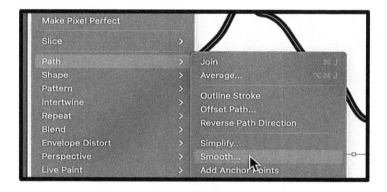

This is going to open up a slider here, where you can adjust the smoothness of your line. There's also the "Auto Smooth" button, but you might prefer to do it manually as it seems to be more effective.

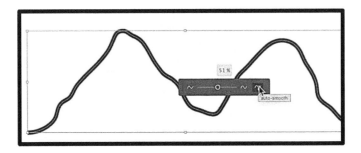

Review Questions

1. What are the primary features and upgrades included in the most recent version of Adobe Illustrator that improve the user experience?

2. How do the latest Adobe Illustrator 2024 improvements help graphic artists increase their workflow efficiency and productivity?

3. Give examples of specific jobs or processes that have been made easier or more effective by the new capabilities introduced in Adobe Illustrator 2024.

CHAPTER 2
GETTING STARTED

If you want to make printables, presentations, SVGs, mockups, and other graphics, Adobe Illustrator is a terrific place to start. In this chapter, we'll start with the basic workspace and then go on to various courses that will teach you how to utilize Adobe Illustrator to create your files. In this chapter, we'll go over why Adobe Illustrator is ideal for creating these files, followed by a walkthrough of the workspace. We'll start by discussing what Illustrator excels at, what it's mediocre at but still used for, and what it's not so good at. We'll then show you how to open it up, create a new file, and explore all of Illustrator's features.

We'll also go over a couple of the tools you'll need to be familiar with, and then we'll get deeper into certain features and tools as we go. Before we begin, we want you to understand that Adobe Illustrator can be frightening; but, if you give yourself the space and time to study, it is a powerful application that will help you to produce stunning designs that can be cut natively.

Some designers are mostly self-taught in Illustrator; they began using it more frequently and eventually became professionals, which is wonderful news for you because it implies you don't need a sophisticated graphic design school to utilize Illustrator. It also means that there are numerous methods to complete all of the steps; it is a matter of determining whatever method works best for you.

Are you ready?

What is Adobe Illustrator?

Illustrator is a vector drawing software, which despite its name, is primarily used for graphic design.

What is a vector? In design, a vector is a picture that can be stretched indefinitely without losing quality. It is the opposite of a bitmap picture, such as a photo, which is made up of pixels and has a fixed resolution. However, bitmap pictures can still be used within Illustrator; it is simply not its strongest suit.

Adobe Illustrator as a vector design software

Before we get into the specifics of our workspace, let's talk about how Adobe Illustrator is a vector design product. This implies that Illustrator operates on points, which we'll refer to as anchor points, and lines, known as pathways. Instead of pixels, this, like Photoshop, may be compatible with photographs, JPEGs, PNGs, and other similar files. They may also be referred to as raster images or bitmaps. The beautiful thing about vectors is that they can be adjusted to any size. You can make them very small or very huge without losing any resolution or quality.

Vector vs. pixels

From our image below, over here on the left we have a vector Popsicle, and then over here on the right we have a pixel Popsicle.

Now, this is already pixelated on the right, but if we zoom in from the left, we can see that no matter how far we zoom in, it does not become pixelated. This is similar to how many fonts function. You can enlarge a typeface and print it on a billboard and it will appear the same as if you printed it on your home printer, because fonts are vector-based, or at least most of them are.

Why is a vector-based system important?

Why is a vector-based system important? Because, when you consider how a cutting machine works, it cuts in lines and turns at points, which is precisely how a vector file is created. When you submit a bitmap pixel image to Cricut Design Space, for example, it will attempt to convert it into a print and then cut it. It will cut around the edge but not include any information. However, if you upload a vector image, such as an SVG, your Cricut will be able to cut it properly.

What you can do with Illustrator

Adobe Illustrator is good for things like illustration and drawing, perfect logo design, branding, illustrators, perfect Flyers, posters, stationary, stickers, icons, fashion, patent making, and sign writing.

What you shouldn't do with Illustrator

Now that you understand what Illustrator is used for, you should be aware that it is unlikely to be the best tool for web design and UI design, owing to the existence of tools such as Figo, XD, and Envision Studio, as well as a plethora of other options. You can create them in Illustrator, but all of the interactivity cannot be added here, so it is best to use those tools. The other things that it's not good at are newsletters, magazines, and books.

Recall that earlier on we said it's good for newsletters, what we mean is small newsletters; the problem with it is Illustrator is designed to do illustration amazingly quickly and beautifully which is great but as soon as you add lots of volume to it like four or eight pages it starts struggling and slowing down especially if you start throwing in lots of big high-quality Images and that is where something like Adobe InDesign comes in.

It does a little bit of what Illustrator does but it allows you to do multiple pages. You can open a 300-page document and InDesign will work perfectly fine but with Illustrator, it becomes extremely slow and annoying so doing a few pages is fine in Illustrator but for lots of pages you need to move to InDesign. Photoshop is another popular tool in the Illustrator group, particularly if you are a designer or book publisher.

Photoshop is used for retouching photographs. Illustrator allows you to make small modifications, edits, and color shifts, but you can't mask anything or cut anyone out because Photoshop does that. Photoshop is used for all types of photo alteration, masking, and cutting. Illustrator does all of the illustrations and makes many small elements, icons, buttons, titles, and drawings, and InDesign is used if it is published in a larger book.

The Welcome Screen

When you first open Illustrator you'll be greeted with the home screen. There are a few presets to choose from, a list of recently opened files, and what's most importantly: the "New file" button.

When you select it, a menu will appear with some settings you may change for your new file, such as size, measurement unit, the number of artboards you want, and advanced choices like Color Mode.

A Quick Tip: Use RGB for anything digital, and CMYK for anything that'll be printed.

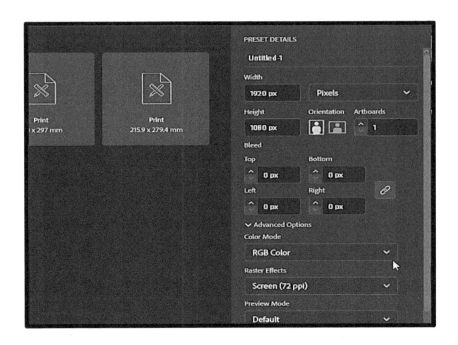

The workspace

After you've completed the setup and clicked the "Create" button, you'll be sent to the program's most crucial feature, the workspace. Everything on the screen, including the tools, menus, and panels, may be changed and moved around.

There are also workspace presets for various workflows, which may be found in Illustrator's top right corner. For the time being, let's use the Essential Classics preset to ensure that we're both on the same page, as well as since this preset is ideal for beginners.

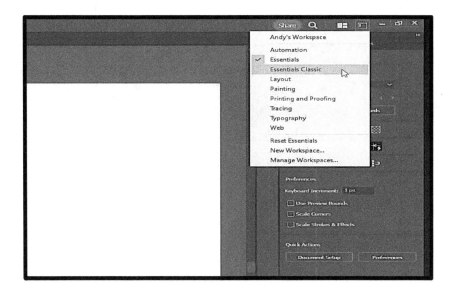

The workspace in Illustrator can be separated into different parts, and knowing them will help you understand the software. On the very top, we have the **Header**. Here, you'll find all the menus. A lot of things in Illustrator can be done in several different ways, but more often than not, you can find what you're looking for in the menus.

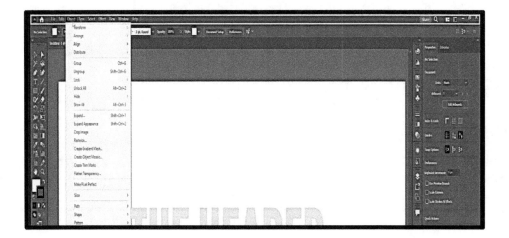

The Control Bar is located down below. It is one of the workspace's most useful parts since it is context-based, which means that its contents alter depending on the object or tool you have selected. For example, when we choose the Text Tool, new options such as font and paragraph emerge.

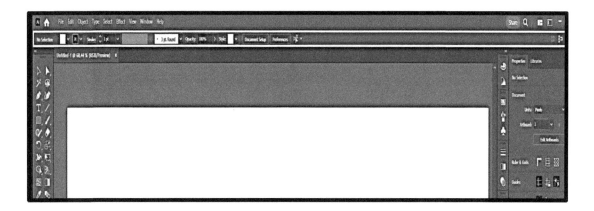

Below the Control Bar, we have the **Document Tabs**. Each tab is a different file you have opened.

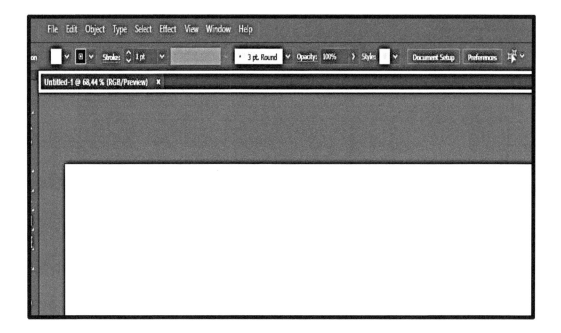

On the left side, we have the Toolbar, which contains all of Illustrator's tools. If you hover your mouse over a tool, Illustrator will display its name, shortcut, and a short movie explaining what it does. If a tool has a small arrow in the corner, you can click and hold it to access comparable tools. For example, clicking and holding the Rectangle Tool opens a menu with similar tools such as the Ellipse Tool and the Polygon Tool.

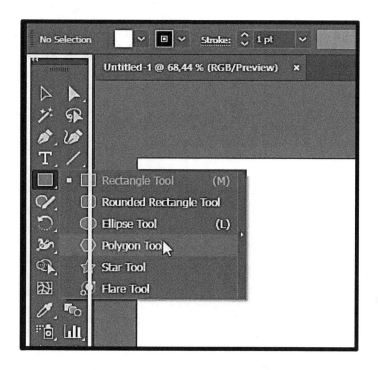

On the right side, we have the panels. Illustrator features multiple panels, each of which is used to execute a distinct operation, such as aligning objects, adjusting gradients, and combining forms. They are all accessible through the Window menu and serve as a complement to the Toolbar. Panels can be enlarged or compressed using the arrow sign in the upper right corner.

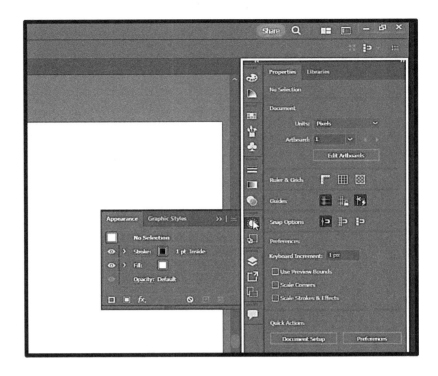

The status bar is located at the bottom of the workspace. It isn't crucial; it displays information about the zoom level, selected artboard, and selected tool. Finally, in the center of it all is the Artboard. This is where you will place items such as geometric shapes, text, and photos. The white rectangle represents the size you chose when creating the document, and multiple artboards can be produced for a multi-page file, such as a presentation. If this is currently overwhelming for you, don't worry; with time, you'll become used to it.

Important tools and panels for starters

Now, we'll show you some of the most important tools and panels to get you started. One of Now, we'll walk you through some of the most crucial tools and panels to get you started. Geometrical shapes are a fundamental component of graphic design, and that is where we will begin. Press the letter M to access the Rectangle Tool. All of the Shape Tools function similarly, so we'll focus on the Rectangle. But remember to click and hold the Rectangle Tool to bring up the menu alongside the other shapes. To construct forms in the artboard, you have two options: click and drag to adjust the shape's size and proportions, or click once to bring up a menu where you may enter the exact size you desire. When clicking and dragging, hold down the SHIFT key to lock the proportions to a perfect square. This also works with various forms, allowing you to make perfect circles or polygons.

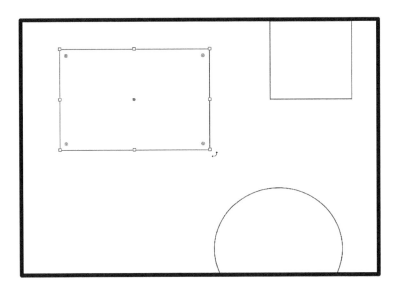

Now that we have something in the Artboard, we can talk about the tool you will use the most: the **Selection Tool**. There are two selection tools - the Selection Tool (keyboard shortcut V), and the Direct Selection Tool, (keyboard shortcut A), or the black cursor and the white cursor.

The Selection Tool (the black cursor) can be used to pick, move, rotate, and scale entire items on the artboard. To move things, simply click and drag them. To rotate, move the cursor close to the corners until it forms this curving two-sided arrow. Use the white squares around the object's bounding box to scale it. If you hold SHIFT while scaling, you will retain the proportions.

Bonus tip: hold the ALT or OPTION key while dragging an object to duplicate it.

How shapes work in Illustrator

Now, before we get started with the Direct Selection Tool (the white pointer), we need to understand how shapes function in Illustrator. Any shape on the Artboard is constructed up of points known as Anchors. A path is formed by connecting two anchors. When the Path is curved, such as in a circle, the Anchor Points will also have Handles to adjust the curvature. These three elements, Anchors, Paths, and Handles, can only be modified individually with the Direct Selection Tool.

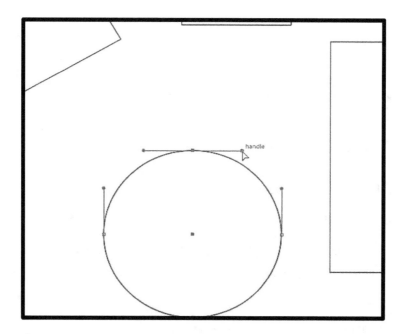

Let us draw a circle on the Artboard. Press the letter L to activate the Ellipse Tool, then click and drag to create a circle. Now, press the letter A to activate the Direct Selection Tool, and hover your cursor over the top section of the circle until the Anchor name appears. Then, click and drag to move only the Anchor Point. Cool, right? You may have noticed that the Handles are also visible now. You can adjust the path's curvature by clicking and dragging them. You can also move a Path by clicking and dragging it, but this can be challenging. What if you wish to draw anything more complicated than geometric shapes? So, you'll use the Pen tool. With the Pen Tool (keyboard shortcut P), each time you click on the Artboard you create an Anchor Point, which will be connected to the previous one, just as you can see in the **image below**.

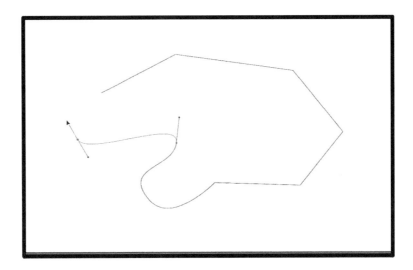

If you click and drag, you'll create a curved path. Clicking back on the first Anchor will close the Path and finish the shape. This tool can be a little bit challenging at first, it requires a little bit of practice to get used to, but it's a super important part of Illustrator and you'll use it a lot once you get the hang of it.

Moving around your workspace

Before we go on to Panels, you should first learn how to navigate the Artboard. Fortunately for you, this is simple. You can move about in a variety of ways, but our suggested techniques are to hold the Spacebar and then click and drag, or to click and drag with the mouse wheel. To zoom, hold the ALT key (or OPTION if you're on a Mac) and scroll with the mouse wheel.

Getting familiar with the panels

Now, let's look at a couple of panels. The Color Panel will be your most frequently used feature. It is already open by default, and some panels do not display all of their options. Click "**Show Options**" from the sandwich menu in the panel's top right corner. That's better.

The Color Panel allows you to modify the color of the shapes you make, both the fill color and the outline color, by simply clicking on their corresponding icons right in the Color Panel. Then, all you have to do is select the object and alter the color to your liking. The Align Panel will be used frequently. It is not open by default, but you can access it through the Window menu. The Align Panel also opens the Pathfinder and Transform Panels, which function together. This panel can be dragged to the right side and docked on the Panel Bar. The Alignment Panel is quite straightforward. Select the object you want to align and select the desired alignment, like center, left, or right. By default, when you select only one object, it will align to the Artboard. But if you have two objects selected, the panel will automatically switch to align to the selection.

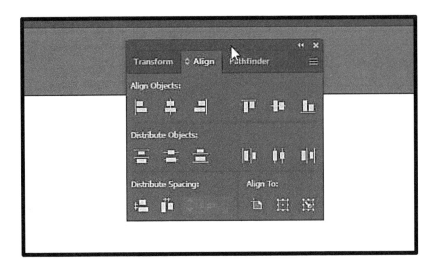

Next in line is the **Pathfinder**. This panel is used to create new shapes by combining two or more shapes. You can unite two shapes into one, intersect the parts that are overlapping, or just divide everything into different shapes. It's really easy and really useful.

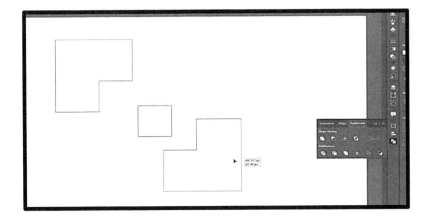

Finally, we have the Properties Panel. This can become your best friend if you get used to it. The Properties Panel, like the Control Bar, is context-based, which means that its contents change depending on what you select. In some ways, the Properties Panel functions similarly to the Control Bar. This is the sole panel that you may need to extend at all times, and it is a true lifesaver because it can accelerate your workflow in a variety of ways.

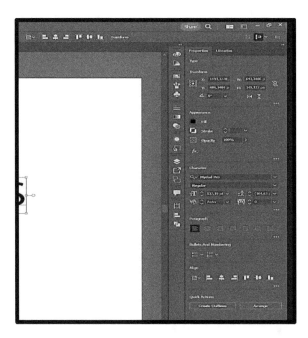

Well, congratulations, you just learned the basics of Illustrator, but your journey is just starting.

Review Questions

1. What is the purpose of Adobe Illustrator and how does it differ from other graphic design software?

2. How can beginners navigate the interface of Adobe Illustrator to start creating their designs?

3. What are the essential tools and functions in Adobe Illustrator that beginners should focus on mastering initially?

CHAPTER 3

GETTING FAMILIAR WITH THE WORK AREA

In this chapter, we're going to do a quick tour around the Illustrator Work area and show you some of the basics to get you started.

Opening a file

First, let's open a file. With Illustrator open, we'll go to File, then "Open" and select the files we've downloaded or saved and wish to open. To open a zip file, simply double-click it. If you don't know how to unzip it, double-click it. If you still can't, search unzipping on your computer and you'll find it.

Creating a new document

To start a new document, use the "New file" button on the left side. Here you can enter your artboard dimensions, color profile, and quality. We'll use an HD artboard with a resolution of 1920 x 1080 pixels to illustrate this.

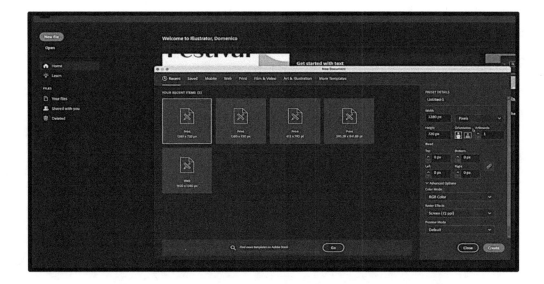

Saving your documents

You can save your document by going to the File menu and clicking "Save as" or using the shortcut COMMAND/CTRL+S.

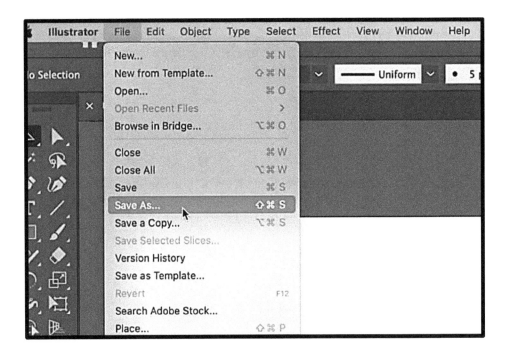

Configuring your workspace

After you open your file, your screen should look similar to what we have in the image below.

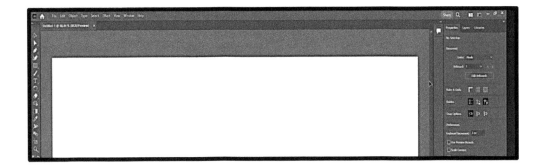

However, if it looks slightly different, there are a few things we'd need you to do to ensure that we're all on the same page as we walk through it. At the top, where it reads Window, go down to "Workspace" and you should be on Essentials. Give it a click, then come back here and reset Essentials to ensure we're all on the same page. The next step is to set the units. Some people prefer centimeters and millimeters; others prefer inches. With nothing chosen, we have a black arrow, which is the default tool that we use. Click on the background in the gray area. This means you have nothing selected and under the Properties tab, depending on where you are, click **on the Properties Tab, and where it says "Units" pick your unit of choice.**

The next thing we're going to do for this course is to make our UI bigger. Currently, you'll notice that everything's quite small and you've got a lot of space but it's not good for these illustrations because you need to see everything and you might find this quite useful if you find everything's just too small to read. Go up to Illustrator, then to Preferences if you're on a Mac but if you're on a PC it's in a slightly different place and that is under the Edit menu, at the bottom here you'll find Preferences so whichever one you're using, go to Preferences and find the option that says User Interface.

We're going to say whether we want it small, medium, or giant. We'll go with Mega Large so you can see it readily as we go, but make sure you choose the size you prefer. It'll indicate we need to restart Illustrator for this to operate, and we'll click OK. When we return to Illustrator, we can see that everything has increased in size.

Navigating the workspace

This opens the Illustrator workspace once you've finished producing your document. The Tools panel is located on the left. We have panels on the right that assist you manage your projects, such as Layers, Colors, Gradients, and more. You can use the spacebar to pan around the artboard. You may also use the Z key on your keyboard to launch the Zoom Tool and zoom in and out of your artwork.

The Layers panel

The Layers panel can be found on the right side of the interface. If you don't find the panel you are looking for head to the Window menu at the top and you can find the list of Property panels.

Layers allow you to keep your designs organized. You can create a new layer, rename them, and even rearrange them however you like.

Creating basic shapes

Let us now show you how to make simple shapes. From the left panel, select the Shape Tool. There are choices for creating rectangles, ellipses, polygons, and other shapes. Select a rectangle tool from this panel, and then click and drag on the artboard to make your shape. Holding SHIFT on your keyboard will result in a perfect square. The same is true when constructing ellipses. To draw a triangle, use the Polygon Tool, click anywhere on the artboard, enter three sides, and then press ENTER.

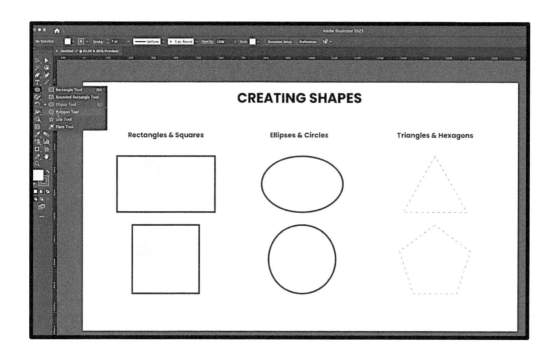

Selecting an object

To choose an object, press the letter V on your keyboard, which opens the Selection Tool. You can then choose your object and drag it around your artboard. To activate the Direct Selection Tool, press the letter A on your keyboard. This tool allows you to choose and adjust points, as well as round off object corners.

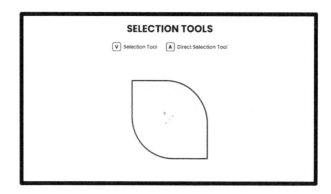

How to Select Multiple Objects

Here's a brief guide to selecting several items in your document. These could be two or more objects, such as forms and text. There are several reasons why you might want to select multiple objects, such as grouping them, aligning them, or applying effects to multiple objects at the same time, but the simplest way to do so is to hold SHIFT while clicking different objects, which will start a group selection.

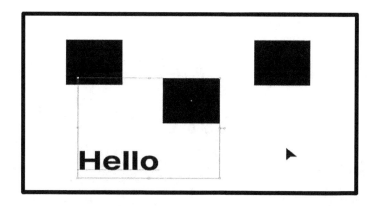

If you accidentally clicked the wrong one, continue to hold SHIFT and it will deselect whatever you click on if you already have that object chosen, making it one of the quickest ways to choose highly precise things. If you wish to choose a large number of things in a certain region, click and drag outside of your objects, and a Marquee will develop, with anything inside that selection selected.

Let's imagine we have two objects selected. We may click and drag to select two more while holding SHIFT, and they will be added to the selection. The same thing applies in reverse; if we wish to deselect two of them, we just click and drag, and they will be deselected. That allows you to select and deselect numerous things at once, rather than holding SHIFT and selecting each one individually. If you toggle down this layer group in your Layers panel, you'll see a single layer with all of the objects on it; it also shows which objects are selected by the little double circle over here, so you can hold SHIFT and click on these layers to select different objects.

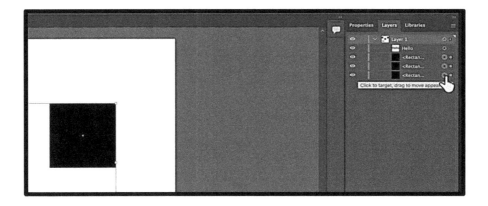

This is a separate method of selecting, whether you hold SHIFT and choose a group of objects in a row or you SHIFT click or COMMAND/CTRL-click on individual objects. As you can see, merely clicking on each of these layers selects the corresponding object. On Windows, holding down the COMMAND or CTRL keys selects numerous objects, while holding down the SHIFT key selects a row of objects. All of these items are out here, so if you had anything named or couldn't quite click on it out here, but you have layers in your Layers panel with these objects, you can select and deselect them over here as well. This is how to select many objects at once in Adobe Illustrator.

Colors and Strokes

With the shapes created, you can assign color fill and color to the strokes by selecting the shape then head to the Color menu and select the color from your swatches to fill.

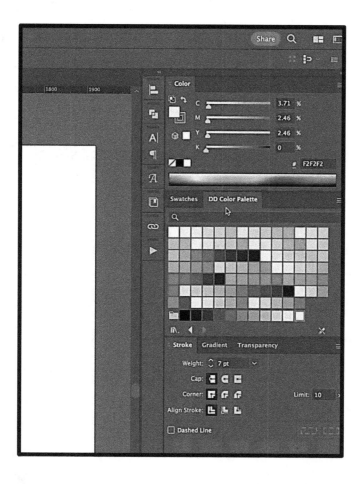

By pressing SHIFT+X on your keyboard you can switch between Fill and Stroke. You can give your shape a thicker stroke by going to the Stroke panel. Here, you can play around with the thickness, the caps, and the corners. The Pen Tool is used to create shapes and paths. Click to create anchor points and drag to create curves. You can also manipulate the curves later on with the Direct Selection Tool.

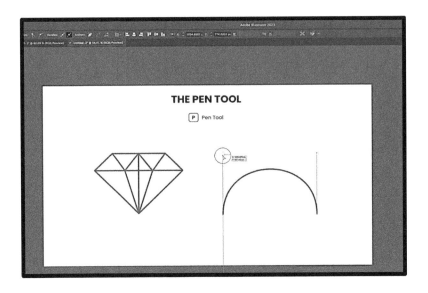

Adding Text

To add text, choose the Type Tool from the Tools panel on the left, then click on the canvas and begin typing. The Character panel allows you to change the font, size, and other settings. If you click and drag on the canvas, an area will be created and filled with example text. The type tool also allows you to type along any path and within any form area.

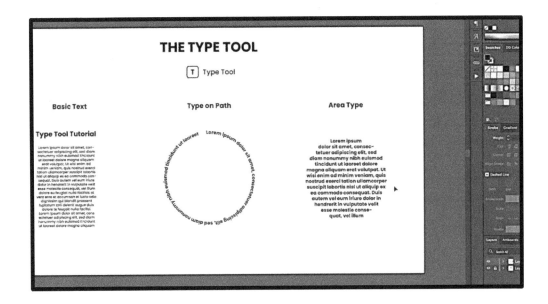

Manipulating Shapes

The Shape Builder Tool is a powerful feature of Adobe Illustrator. It lets you combine, subtract, and split shapes to make your vector images. To enable the Shape Builder Tool, select multiple shapes and then press SHIFT+M on your keyboard. To combine the forms, pick this tool and then click and drag over gray areas. To subtract shapes, hold down ALT for Windows or OPTION for Mac and click or drag over the sections you want to erase.

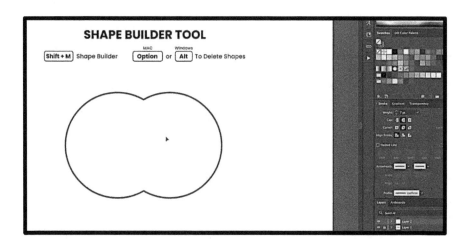

Sampling object attributes

The Eyedropper Tool allows you to easily sample strokes, colors, and other properties from one object to another. You can use the tool by pressing the letter I on your keyboard. To sample a color and stroke from one shape to another, select a new shape and use the Eyedropper to click on the other shapes.

Apply color transitions

The Gradient Tool lets you add color transitions to objects and shapes. Select any object and go to the Gradient panel; you may apply a linear, rounded, or freeform gradient. Once you've chosen one, use the letter G on your keyboard to open a gradient line popup where you may adjust the gradient in any way you want.

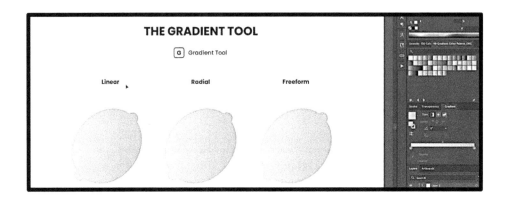

Isolation mode

The second thing we'd want to show you is something called Isolation mode, which is where many individuals become lost very quickly. We're going to attach an artboard to the window, then combine a few items and show you where you're likely to get lost. We'll go to our Selection Tool, click once, hold down the SHIFT key on our keyboard, and click once to choose multiple items. So we're holding SHIFT down the entire time and clicking a variety of stuff to move. We've got them all chosen; we're going to group them, so over here in our Properties panel, there's a group option, or you can right-click it and select the group. Now they are grouped, but if you enjoy double-clicking, you will enter the indicated region, so if we click on this, it is one unit, but if we double-click it, everything else is washed away and no longer works. How are we going out? To exit Isolation mode, simply double-click on the background. So double-click to enter, and double-click to exit. That's where you might get stuck. This has to do with things that are grouped and if you double-click things you'll end up in there so double-click to get in or with the little arrow here you can go back and it just takes you out as well.

41

Review Questions

1. How can you create a new document in Adobe Illustrator, including specifying dimensions and resolution?

2. How can the workspace be configured to suit your individual preferences?

3. What are the different panels available in Adobe Illustrator and how can they be used effectively during the design process?

CHAPTER 4

GETTING TO KNOW ALL ADOBE ILLUSTRATOR TOOLS

This chapter covers all the tools you'll find in Adobe Illustrator with a detailed explanation of what they do.

The Selection Tool

This is the most essential Illustrator tool, and it will be the one you use the most. The shortcut is the letter V. It allows you to select entire objects, groups, and clipping masks by clicking or dragging. This tool also allows you to move, resize, rotate, and round corners.

The Direct Selection Tool

The letter A represents a keyboard shortcut. It allows you to select and move specific pathways, anchor points, and handles. It also selects individual items within groups or clipping masks, which have a fill that may be clicked on. Rounding corners is also feasible.

The Group Selection Tool

There is no default shortcut for this tool. It is used to select objects inside a group without having to ungroup them.

The Magic Wand Tool

The keyboard shortcut is the letter Y. It is used to pick items that share similar features, such as color and stroke. It selects any object in your document, even those in groups and clipping masks. The Magic Wand panel allows you to adjust the options for your magic wand.

The Lasso Tool

The keyboard shortcut is the letter Q. It selects any anchor points inside the path drawn, including from objects in groups and clipping masks.

The Pen Tool

The keyboard shortcut is the letter P. It is used for drawing pathways. Each click adds a new anchor point to the path, and moving the mouse before releasing the click creates curvature handles. The trail can be closed by clicking back on the first anchor.

The Add Anchor Point Tool

The keyboard shortcut is the plus symbol (+). It adds a new anchor point to a path.

The Delete Anchor Point Tool

The keyboard shortcut is the minus (-) symbol. It removes an anchor point from a path.

Bonus tip: if you hold the shift key while removing the anchor point, the path will be recalculated to stay the same.

The Anchor Point Tool

The keyboard shortcut is SHIFT+C. It allows you to add, remove, or edit handles on anchor points. Clicking on a curved anchor point removes the handles, but clicking and dragging restores them. Dragging one handle with this tool moves it independently of the other.

The Curvature Tool

The keyboard shortcut is SHIFT+TILDE. It is similar to the Pen Tool, but automatically creates curved paths.

The Type Tool

The keyboard shortcut is the letter T. This tool allows you to add text by clicking anywhere. Textboxes can be created by clicking and dragging. To edit existing text, simply click on top of it.

The Area Type Tool

This doesn't have any default shortcut. With this tool, you can click on a path to create text inside it.

The Type on a Path Tool

This doesn't have any default shortcut. With this tool, click on a path to create text that follows the path.

The Vertical Type Tool

There is no default shortcut. With this tool, click anywhere to create vertical text.

The Vertical Area Type Tool

There is no default shortcut. With this tool, click on a path to create vertical text inside it.

The Vertical Type on a Path Tool

There is no default shortcut. With this tool, click on a path to create a vertical text that follows the path.

The Touch Type Tool

The keyboard shortcut is SHIFT+T. This functions identically to the Selection Tool but with individual characters from a text. Clicking on a character displays the bounding box, which can then be scaled, moved, or rotated.

The Line Segment Tool

The keyboard shortcut is the backslash. With this tool, click and drag to create a line.

The Arc Tool

There is no default shortcut. Using this tool, click and drag to create an arc.

The Spiral Tool

There are no preset shortcuts. Create a spiral by clicking and dragging this tool. To modify the amount of cycles in the spiral, use the up and down arrow keys.

The Rectangular Grid Tool

There is no default shortcut. Using this tool, click and drag to create a rectangular grid. Use the arrow keys to change the number of columns and lines.

The Polar Grid Tool

There is no default shortcut. Using this tool, click and drag to create a polar grid. Use the arrow keys to change the number of subdivisions.

The Rectangle Tool

The keyboard shortcut is the letter M. Click and drag to form a rectangle. Holding SHIFT will result in a flawless square.

The Rounded Rectangle Tool

There is no default shortcut. Click and drag to create a rounded rectangle. Holding SHIFT will create a perfect square. Use the up or down arrow keys to change the roundness.

The Ellipse Tool

The keyboard shortcut is the letter L. Click and drag to create an ellipse. Holding SHIFT will create a perfect circle.

The Polygon Tool

There are no preset shortcuts. Click and drag to form a polygon with all sides the same size. To alter the number of sides, use the up or down arrow keys.

The Star Tool

There are no preset shortcuts. Click and drag to form a star. To modify the number of points, use the up or down arrow keys. Hold CMD or CTRL while dragging to adjust the size of the arms.

The Flare Tool

There are no preset shortcuts. Click and drag to form the light rays and halo, then click in the direction you want to add the light rings. The objects generated already have blending modes set, so you may just drop the flare on top of a picture or illustration.

The Paintbrush Tool

The keyboard shortcut is the letter B. Click and drag to create a smooth path, which is more like a hand-drawn style. Holding ALT after you start dragging the mouse will create a closed path. Press the square bracket keys to change the brush size.

The Blob Brush Tool

The keyboard shortcut is SHIFT+B. Create a filled compound path by clicking and dragging. If two pathways with the same appearance come into contact, they combine. To alter the brush size, press the square bracket keys.

The Shaper Tool

The shortcut is SHIFT+N. Click and drag to draw a rough approximation of the shape you desire, and Illustrator will automatically turn it into a crisp geometric shape. It works for straight lines, rectangles, ellipses, and polygons.

The Pencil Tool

The keyboard shortcut is the letter N. It works very similarly to the Paintbrush Tool. Click and drag to create smooth paths. Dragging the mouse close to where you started will close the path.

The Smooth Tool

There are no preset shortcuts. To smooth out a specified path, click and drag over it. It's also a good approach to reduce the amount of anchor points.

The Path Eraser Tool

There is no default shortcut. Click and drag over a selected path to erase parts of it. This tool is terrible to use.

The Join Tool

There is no default shortcut. Select two open paths, then click and drag to join them.

The Eraser Tool

The keyboard shortcut is SHIFT+E. Click and drag on top of a selected object to erase parts of it. Press the square bracket keys to change the eraser size.

The Scissors Tool

The keyboard shortcut is the letter C. Click on a path to split it at that specific point.

The Knife Tool

There is no default shortcut. Click and drag over an object to cut it.

The Rotate Tool

The keyboard shortcut is the letter R. To rotate the selected object, simply click and drag it. To adjust the rotation's reference point, click anywhere on the artboard. Holding SHIFT will lock the rotation in 45-degree increments.

The Reflect Tool

The keyboard shortcut is the letter O. Click and drag to reflect the selected object. This tool can be quite confusing, the easiest way to use it is to hold shift and drag observing the reference point.

The Scale Tool

The keyboard shortcut is the letter S. To scale the selected object, simply click and drag it. Holding SHIFT locks the scale horizontally, vertically, or proportionally, depending on which direction you drag. Clicking anywhere on your artboard will alter the reference point.

The Shear Tool

There are no preset shortcuts. Click and drag to distort the selected object. Clicking anywhere on the artboard changes the reference point, and holding SHIFT locks the tool to the horizontal or vertical axis.

The Reshape Tool

There is no default shortcut. Click and drag on a path to reshape it. This tool is clunky and can add lots of anchor points. There are better ways to reshape paths.

The Width Tool

The keyboard shortcut is SHIFT+W. Click and drag on a stroke to adjust its width at that point. The Width Tool adds handles that can be moved and edited whenever you want.

The Warp Tool

The keyboard shortcut is SHIFT+R. Click and drag to deform a path in the direction you drag.

The Twirl Tool

There is no default shortcut. Click and hold to twirl the object around the center of the brush.

The Pucker Tool

There is no default shortcut. Click and hold to deform the path towards the center of the brush.

The Bloat Tool

There are no preset shortcuts. To distort the route to the outside of the brush, click and hold. It is the antithesis of the Pucker Tool.

The Scallop Tool

There is no default shortcut. Click and hold to **scallop** the path towards the center of the brush.

The Crystalize Tool

There is no default shortcut. Click and hold to deform the object towards the outside of the brush, creating spikes. It's the opposite of the Scallop Tool.

The Wrinkle Tool

There is no default shortcut. Click and hold to wrinkle the path by deforming it randomly.

The Free Transform Tool

The keyboard shortcut is the letter E. When you pick this tool while an item is selected, you will get a menu with three options: free transform, perspective distort, and free distortion. This tool allows you to scale, rotate, shear, and add perspective to any object.

The Puppet Warp Tool

There are no preset shortcuts. When an object is selected, this tool will bring up a mesh that can be used to distort it. The mesh has control points that can be dragged and rotated. They can be removed by selecting them and using the Delete key, or inserted by clicking on the mesh. This tool does not add anchor points, therefore it can only deform existing anchors.

The Shape Builder Tool

The keyboard shortcut is SHIFT+N. Click and drag through multiple paths to unite them in a single shape. Hold ALT and drag to delete paths. This tool works similarly to the Pathfinder.

The Live Paint Bucket Tool

The keyboard shortcut is the letter M. To create a live paint group, select multiple objects and click the Live Paint Bucket icon. After that, click on any contained path to paint it with the chosen color. The swatches window also allows you to select a color palette and switch between colors using the left and right arrow keys.

The Live Paint Selection Tool

The keyboard shortcut is SHIFT+L. It is used to select fills and strokes inside a live paint group. Each click will select either the fill, or the stroke, and not both, like a normal selection. Hold SHIFT then select more than one stroke or fill.

The Perspective Grid Tool

The keyboard shortcut is SHIFT+P. Selecting this tool opens the Perspective Grid in the artboard. The grid's various control points allow you to modify the angles. While the grid is active in the artboard, objects will appear on a specified side of the viewpoint. The side can be changed using the icon that appears in the corner of the screen while the grid is active, or by using the shortcuts numbered 1, 2, 3, and 4. To collapse the grid, pick the Perspective Grid Tool and click the X in the icon. The number of perspective points can also be changed in the Perspective Grid menu.

The Perspective Selection Tool

The keyboard shortcut is SHIFT+V. This lets you move things within the perspective. Moving objects with this tool will automatically scale and distort them to maintain perspective. When moving an object, you can use the shortcuts 1, 2, or 3 to change the viewpoint side.

The Mesh Tool

The keyboard shortcut is the letter U. Click on a selected object to create a color mesh. Each click adds a new point to the mesh, which can be painted a different color.

The Gradient Tool

The keyboard shortcut is the letter G. Click and drag on an object that is painted with a gradient to adjust the angle and position of the gradient, as well as the position of colors and transitions.

The Eyedropper Tool

The keyboard shortcut is the letter I. With an object selected, use the Eyedropper to duplicate the colors of another object. If you hold down the SHIFT key, the stroke or fill color will be utilized, depending on where you click. The Eyedropper also copies transparency and text characteristics.

The Measure Tool

There is no default shortcut. Click and drag to measure a distance in the artboard. The info panel will be opened. The panel shows the position of the start point, the width and height distances, the distance in a straight line, and the angle of the measurement.

The Blend Tool

The keyboard shortcut is the letter W. Click on two or more objects to combine their shapes and colors. Objects are grouped when the mix is produced, but they can still be picked with the Direct Selection or Group Selection Tools.

The Symbol Sprayer Tool

The keyboard shortcut is SHIFT+S. Select a symbol from the Symbols panel and spray it onto the artboard to generate many instances of that symbol. To create a new symbol, simply drag the desired vector into the Symbols panel. All instances of the symbol will be grouped into a Symbol Set.

The Symbol Shifter Tool

There is no default shortcut. With a Symbol set selected, click and drag to shift the symbols inside the group.

The Symbol Scruncher Tool

There is no default shortcut. With a Symbol Set selected, click and hold on a symbol to bring the other symbols close to it. To bring them far apart, hold the ALT key before clicking.

The Symbol Sizer Tool

There are no preset shortcuts. With a Symbol Set selected, click to enlarge the symbols within the brush area. The closer a symbol is to the brush's center, the larger it will seem. Holding ALT when clicking causes the symbols to scale down.

The Symbol Spinner Tool

There is no default shortcut. With a Symbol Set selected, click and drag close to the center of a symbol to spin it.

The Symbol Stainer Tool

There are no preset shortcuts. With a Symbol Set and a color selected, click on the symbols to paint them with the chosen color. The amount of paint applied depends on how close you are to the center of the brush and how long you hold the click.

The Symbol Screener Tool

There is no default shortcut. With a Symbol Set selected, click on the symbols to make them transparent. Proximity to the center of the brush and how long you hold the click affects how transparent they'll be.

The Symbol Styler Tool

There is no default shortcut. With a Symbol Set and a graphic style selected, click on the symbols to apply the style to them. Proximity to the center of the brush and how long you hold the click affect how strongly the style will be applied.

The Graph Tools

All of the graph tools work in the same way, so we'll go over them all together. The first graph tool, the Column Graph Tool, has a keyboard shortcut of the letter J. Click and drag anywhere on the artboard to construct a graph of the desired size. A spreadsheet will emerge, allowing you to enter the data that will be shown in the graph. External data input is also an option.

The Artboard Tool

The keyboard shortcut is SHIFT+O. This allows you to create, move, copy, and edit artboards in your document.

The Slice Tool

The keyboard shortcut is SHIFT+K. To create a rectangle slice, click and drag on the artboard. The artboard will be divided into chunks, which can be exported independently via the "Save for Web" menu option.

The Slice Selection Tool

There is no default shortcut. This allows you to select, move, and resize slices.

The Hand Tool

The keyboard shortcut is the letter H. Click and drag to move across the artboard. You can also rapidly access the Hand Tool by holding the Space key and clicking and dragging, or by clicking and dragging with the mouse wheel. When you release the mouse click in any case, you will be returned to the previously utilized tool.

The Rotate View Tool

The keyboard shortcut is SHIFT+H. Click and drag to rotate the view in Illustrator. Holding SHIFT will lock the rotation in increments of 15 degrees.

The Print Tiling Tool

There are no preset shortcuts. Selecting this tool activates the visibility of printed tiles. By default, your artboard will contain simply one tile. To tile your document for printing, enter the Print menu and choose "Tile full pages" or "Tile imageable areas" from the Scaling drop-down menu.

This will tile your document in the specified media size. Select "**Done.**" You will now have many tiles that can be repositioned using the Print Tiling Tool.

The Zoom Tool

The keyboard shortcut is the letter Z. Select to zoom in. Hold ALT and click to zoom out. Touching and dragging sideways allows for smooth zooming in and out. All of these tools are for Adobe Illustrator. Many of the tools described in this chapter have additional capabilities and behaviors that you will discover as you gain experience with Illustrator.

Also, almost every tool's behavior changes whether you hold the SHIFT, ALT, or CTRL/CMD keys, so try them all. Many of these tools will open customization menus when you press the ENTER key with the tool chosen, so explore that as well.

Review Questions

1. Explain 7 tools in Adobe Illustrator and give examples of how they are used.

2. How can you customize your toolbar in Adobe Illustrator to easily access your favorite tools?

3. Are there any lesser-known tools in Adobe Illustrator that can make the design process better? If so, how do you use them?

CHAPTER 5

CREATING A GREAT-LOOKING LOGO DESIGN

In this chapter, we are going to share with you the secrets behind creating a great-looking logo design. We'll be looking at the tools, techniques, and a few things to watch out for now.

Make a simple logo with shapes.

The logo we'll be developing is a large letter S with gradients, but if you're following along, you can use any letter you choose. With a fresh document open, select the Ellipse Tool, then click and drag while holding SHIFT to make a circle. We'll drag while holding ALT or OPTION to duplicate and scale it up, then select everything and set the Fill to None. To create a line, we'll pull the top section up a little bit, select the Line Tool, and click while holding SHIFT.

Line up objects

First, we're going to look at lining up objects so we are going to select everything and align these centrally then holding SHIFT, we can move these up and down so the lines all connect.

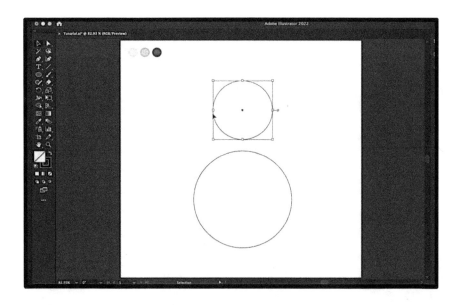

Holding SHIFT allows us to use the primary Selection Tool to expand this line, and if we zoom in closely, we can try to match up the circle even more closely with this line. If we hit COMMAND or CTRL+Y, we can enter Outline mode and select the Direct Selection Tool. We can then use this to move the Anchor Point out of the way, bring it back, and it will snap to the route. When moving this around, make sure the line does not overlap the circle.

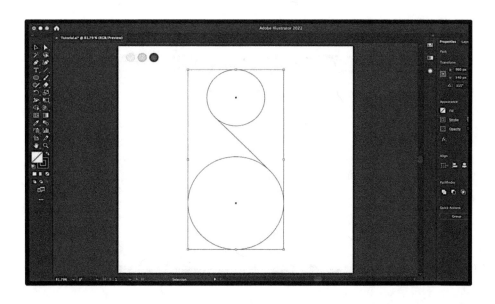

Let's do the same thing for the other end and the goal is to line these up precisely so we get a smooth letter S. Now we are going to thicken up that stroke a bit so it looks better.

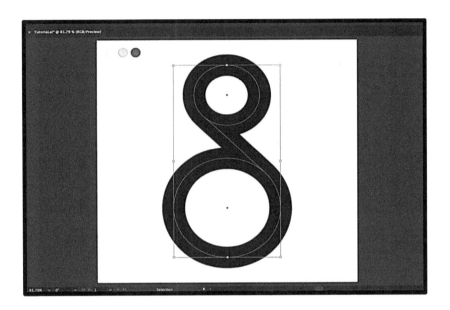

Make some cuts

Now it's time to make some Cuts along the path. We are going to select the Scissor Tool usually hidden under the Eraser Tool and we can click anywhere on a path to cut. By adding these cuts, we get more anchor points.

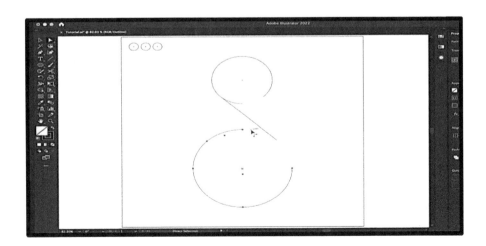

Remove anchor points

We're going to remove these anchor points, so go back to Outline mode and click between two anchor points to pick the path, then press Delete or Backspace. If we do it again, it eliminates too much, so we'll undo it; make sure to erase any stray anchor points that you detect.

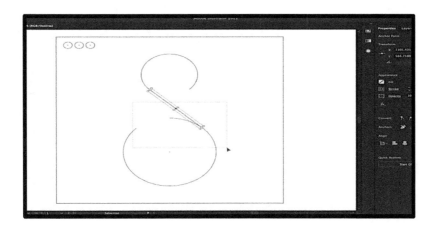

Now let's do the same for the bottom, which means we are going to drag over that segment and press delete or backspace. Make sure you get rid of any straight anchor points and then we can look at removing and merging segments so we nearly have a letter S.

Remove and merge segments.

We'll drag over everything, then pick the Shape Builder Tool, hold ALT or OPTION, and then drag over a route to eliminate it. We need to zoom in on where the pathways join and to do so, we need to make a little intersection. At this point, our smart guides are snapping this to something annoying, so we can turn them off with COMMAND or CTRL+U. We can now make this intersection slightly, and if you have trouble selecting the path you want, simply press COMMAND or CTRL+2 to lock one path, select the other, and then unlock them. Right now we know these paths are touching, we are going to select everything, grab the Shape Builder Tool, hold ALT or OPTION, and drag. Now if you've done this correctly you should have three separate pieces and we're going to join the paths together.

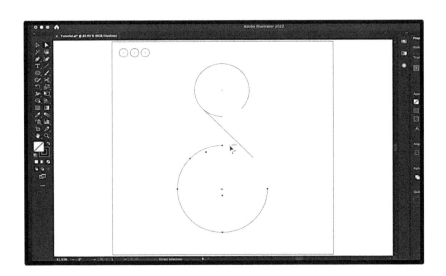

Join the paths together.

Drag over the end anchor points with the Direct Selection Tool, then go to Object, then "Path" and "Join." Repeat for the opposite end, resulting in a single long path with rounded strokes.

Round off the stroke

We'll change the Cap type to round from the Stroke drop-down menu, which will smooth down those sharp edges. If you want to trim them down, simply use the Scissor Tool to make a cut and then delete the end anchor point.

Extend paths

We may use the Pen Tool to expand a line by selecting an existing anchor point, holding SHIFT, and clicking. We aren't using this strategy this time, but we wanted to show it because it is quite valuable. We are going to deepen the stroke and pare down the top section slightly more.

Expand strokes

Let's look at enlarging Strokes; with everything chosen, go to Object, then "Expand." Leave fill and stroke checked, then click OK to convert a stroke into a shape with a solid fill. Now, using the Eyedropper Tool, we may sample the light green and proceed to the following stage.

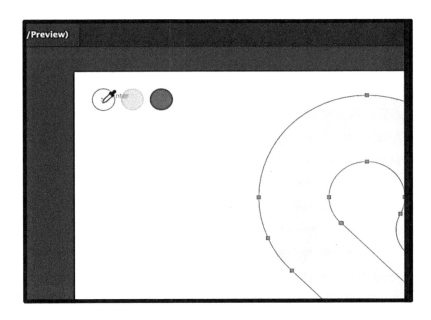

Use shapes to define new segments.

Once again, let's select the Ellipse Tool and create a circle. We are going to make sure we have no fill and a stroke (making that stroke the darkest green) and we're going to adjust the size and position. We can then jump into Outline mode, zoom in nicely and closely, and line everything up precisely and the more you zoom in the better the result.

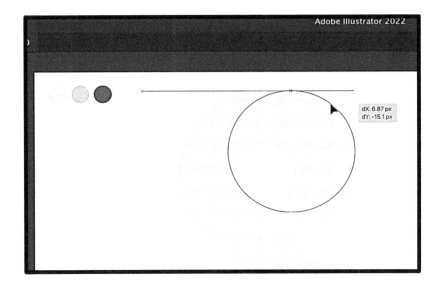

Separate shapes

Let's look at dividing shapes. We'll select everything, then go to Edit, then "Copy" and "Paste" in position. Hold SHIFT and use the right arrow key to nudge the second form out, then pick the first shape, grab the form Builder Tool, and hold ALT or OPTION while clicking and dragging through some of the top segments to remove them.

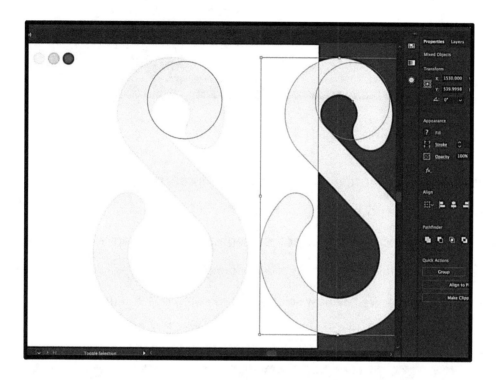

Now we need to do the exact reverse with the second shape, so let's begin by deleting the unnecessary portions, and after that's done, you can let go of ALT or OPTION and just click and drag across the remaining segments. We can then use SHIFT and the left Arrow key to nudge this back into place. We'll give this extra part the darkest green and repeat for the bottom. Simply eliminate any remaining path segments.

Apply custom gradients

Now let's apply some custom gradients. First, choose the main body and open the Gradient panel. Then, click on the slider to add the default gradient, double-click the black switch to the Swatches tab, and select the deepest green. Click anywhere on the slider to add a new color. For this, we'll choose the middle green, double-click the white, and then add the lightest green. We can now select the darker regions and use the Eyedropper tool to sample the same gradient.

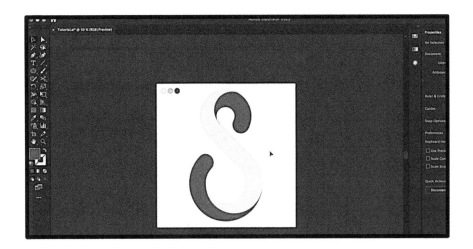

This does look a bit off so we are going to change the angle of this gradient, that way, we get the darker color on the left and just by doing this, it makes a big difference. Now for that main body section, we are going to add a few more swatches and we'll have that lighter green right in the middle acting as a highlight. We are also going to adjust the angle and then delete these three swatches.

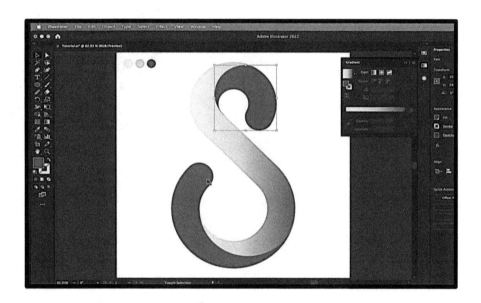

Get highlights included

Now it's time to provide some highlights. First, we'll zoom out and then select the main body, hold SHIFT, and use the left Arrow key to nudge the new shapes out, add another copy to the right-hand side, and with the left one selected, set the fill color to none and then make the stroke a bright right color (we'll go with magenta), and the goal here is to use the Direct Selection Tool to delete all of the anchor points except the ones where we want the highlight.

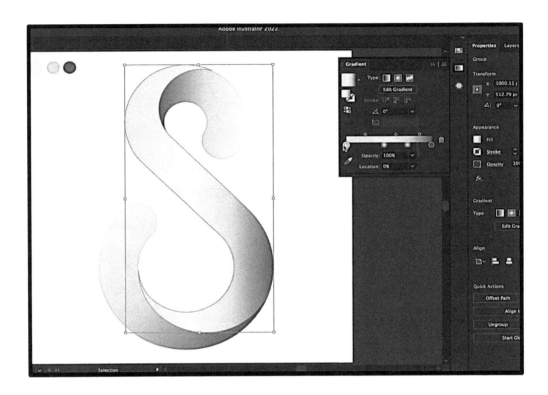

Once we've separated those anchor points, we can nudge them back into position and zoom in close. If you have problems selecting this path, simply nudge those other pieces out of the way, and to make things easier, select the pink curve and make sure it is at the front. Now let's thicken that stroke, and then use the Stroke panel to adjust the width profile to something pleasant, which will give us a good shape for the highlight. We'll now put everything back together and experiment with different blending modes.

Blend altogether

Of course, we don't want this to be pink so we can select it and sample a different color like the gradient for example or we could just pick a color like white.

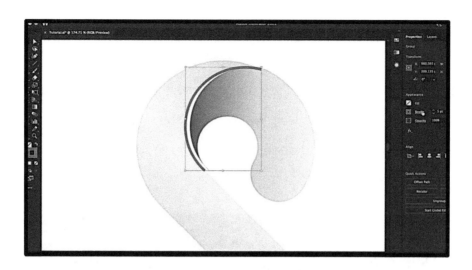

Now let's go and expand the appearance so the shape has a solid fill. If we hop into Outline mode we can see this shape has a line down the middle and if we start using blending modes to reduce the opacity we'll be able to see where the other shapes underneath meet and it will look a bit terrible so we are going to copy the top section and nudge it out, drag over everything to select, grab the Shape Builder Tool hold ALT or OPTION and click and drag over everything and then remove just one half of that curve.

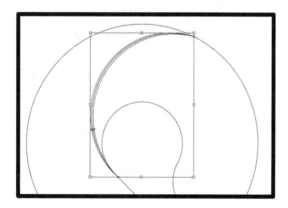

We can also trim off the ends if they are somewhat too fine, and by reducing half of this form, we have made the Highlight narrower. If you want a thicker highlight, just make sure to account for it earlier in the process when setting the stroke width. Now let's delete that solid white one and then nudge back in the new highlight. Because this doesn't bridge where the two shapes underneath meet, we can change the blending mode to something like overlay or soft light, and we can see that this effect looks cool because the colors of the logo underneath are visible as well. We are to do the same again and add a highlight to the bottom. After all is said and done, you should have something that looks like what we have in the **image below**.

Design Modern Logo Using Grid

In this part, we'll show you how to create a logo using any individual letter. We will also walk you through the entire process of making your logo current. First, we'll type the letter M, which will be our design. Make sure you're using the Asgaard font, then use the Line Segment Tool to make a line. Give it a stroke color, then select and copy the line while holding ALT, and finally hit D to create a total of four lines.

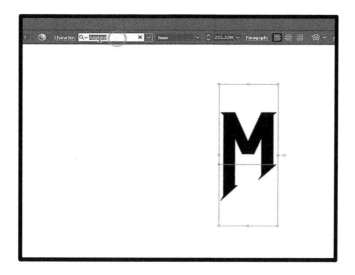

Now select the lines and group them. Now we need to copy the lines so go to the Edit menu and select Copy. Again, go to the Edit menu and select "Paste in place." Now rotate the line 90 degrees.

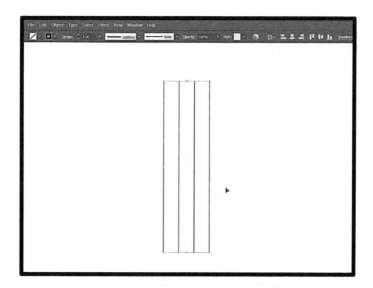

Next, select the lines, copy them, and move them a little bit aside. You can easily copy it by pressing CTRL+C and CTRL+F. After that, select the top line and make it smaller, changing the color as well.

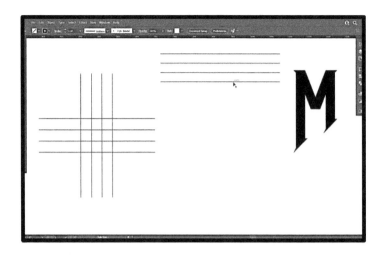

You can add the red lines to the other lines, then pick the red lines, go to Transform, and rotate 123 degrees. Select both lines and group them. After that, select everything and align it in the center. Then, select the red lines and reflect the rotated ones. To reflect, right-click your mouse and pick Transform, then "Reflect" and copy it.

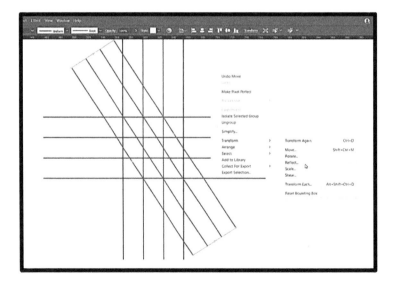

Now we are designing our end letter on these lines but before that, we have to check whether the top line is perfect or not so we'll go to Outline mode by pressing CTRL+Y.

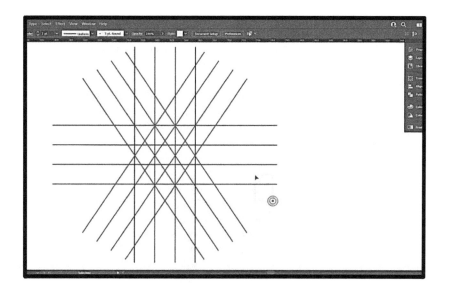

As we can see from the image above, there is a small gap, which we will match. We can now return to regular mode by pressing CTRL+Y, choosing the lines, ungrouping them, and making them somewhat longer. At this point, we will select everything, then use the Shape Builder Tool and turn on the Fill color. We'll draw the letter M.

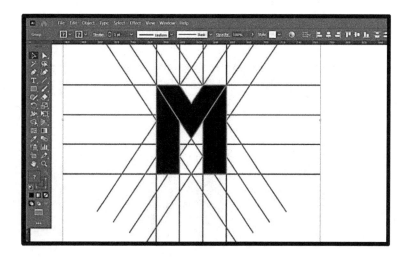

After we have successfully drawn the letter M we are going to move it above the lines but first, we have to ungroup it so we'll hold SHIFT, select the letter M, and move it above the lines. We can now turn off the stroke color of the letter M letter, then select the design and make it a group.

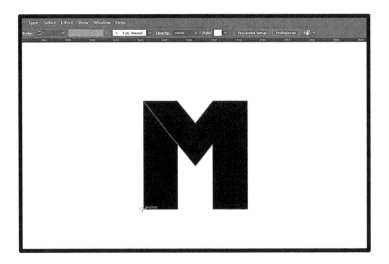

We'll use the Rectangle Tool to design a rectangle that looks like the letter M, then modify the color of the rectangle. We can also reduce the opacity. From there, we would select the rectangle, double-click on the curve point, and curve it as desired, then reflect the curve using the way we demonstrated earlier.

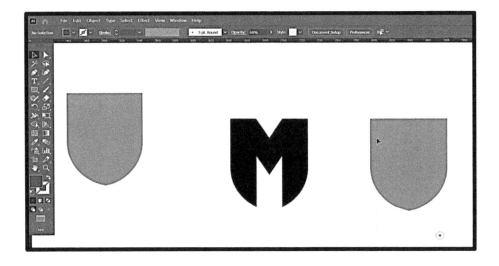

Select everything, take the Shape Builder Tool, and delete it. Next, move the rectangle above the design. Select the shield and change the color from fill to stroke color then change the color to black.

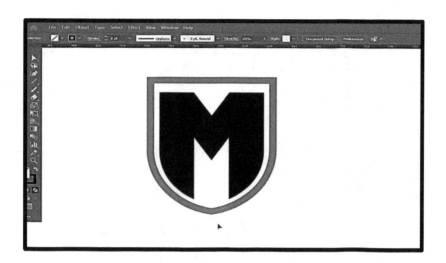

Select everything and set the alignment to center. Select the shield and enlarge it. We can also change the stroke color. Next, choose the shield; then go to Object and select "Path," followed by "Outline Path." Select the pattern, then use the Eyedropper Tool to apply the color of your choosing. Draw a rectangle the same size as the artboard and send it back.

Now take the Pen Tool and draw the middle of the shape. We can also decrease the opacity of the part.

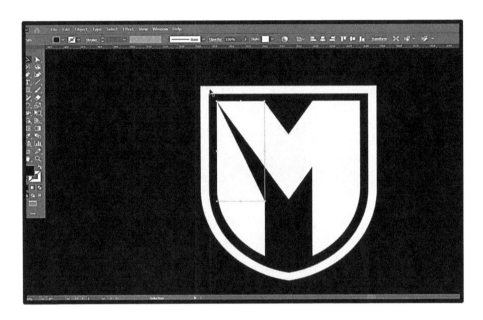

Select the part and reflect it by using the method we showed you then place it perfectly over the middle part. With that, we have completed our logo design.

Review Questions

1. What should you think about when creating a good-looking logo in Adobe Illustrator?

2. Give step-by-step instructions on how to use shapes, text, and effects to make a logo in Adobe Illustrator.

3. How can you make sure your logo looks professional and can be made bigger or smaller without losing quality?

CHAPTER 6

HOW TO MANAGE AND WORK WITH ARTBOARDS

Understanding how to maintain and work with artboards is critical for learning the fundamentals of Illustrator. Working with artboards is an important step in learning how to utilize Illustrator more efficiently. Artboards can speed up your workflow by scaling and rearranging them, so in this chapter, we'll look at how to manage and deal with them in Illustrator. A lot of times clients will ask for multiple versions of things and you want to make sure that they are happy so in this section, we are going to be looking at how to navigate, create, and edit artboards in Adobe Illustrator and then use these new skills to create design options for a holiday greeting card.

What is an Artboard?

An Artboard is the area that we are working on and will appear when we export, so think of it as windows. If we have a bunch of different shapes that we are working on, the gray line we see on the interface is the artboard, so if we click on it, it will turn black, indicating that it is now the active artboard; however, if we click on another one, the previous artboard will turn gray, and the new one will turn black.

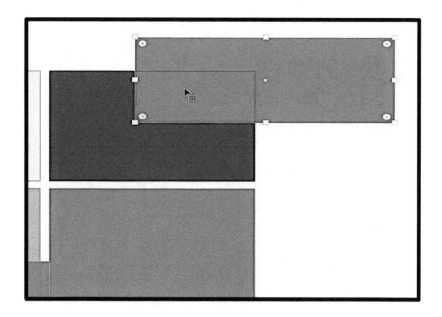

What is necessary to know is that the black outline of an artboard is the active one that you are currently engaged in. The reason you need to know what you're working on is that if you select a shape and then align it to an artboard and start using your Alignment tools, it will align to the active artboard, so make sure that the artboard you want is active before you align to it. Another thing we want you to know about artboards is that you may create as many as you like within the project, and they can be scaled and altered as needed.

Making changes to the Artboard

Now that you've generated a 1080 × 1080 artboard, let's imagine you want to change its size, position, or shape. There are a few options for doing it. The first option is to use the Artboard Tool from the Toolbar, or to hit SHIFT+O on the keyboard.

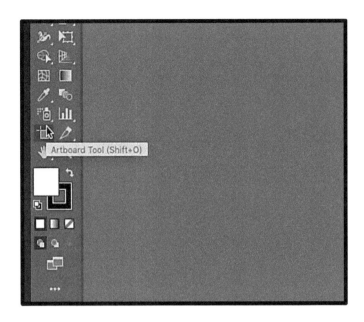

If you click on that, the bounding box for the artboard will appear, and you can simply drag on the anchor points of the bounding box to resize it. You'll also notice a little pop-up showing the size of the artboard, so if you need it in a specific size, you can get it that way, but if you need something a little more precise, there are a couple of different ways that you can do that, one of which is to use the Artboard properties in the Toolbar.

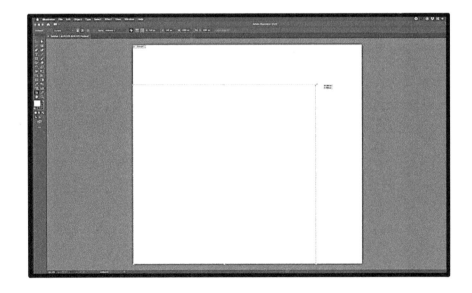

Changing the color of your artboard

We can change colors and adapt this to the way that we want it to look. If we want one that is all one color we can select the Artboard and just use the Eyedropper Tool to make it nice and bright. We can play around and do whatever you want with these artboards.

Artboard Properties

Depending on how Illustrator is configured, you may find them in the Properties panel on the right or, if enabled, in the control bar at the top. If you don't have either of these choices enabled, you can locate them under Window, where the Control is at the top and the Properties are on the right. With these, you can key in particular values for the width and height of the artboard, including the specific size that you want, so if you're looking for the 4 x 5 ratio for Instagram, you can modify it to 1350 and you'll have the artboards ready for your 4 by 5 post. You can also change the position of your artboard using the x and the y values on both these menus. You even have the option to choose from a specific template if you want a preset for the artboard size so if you're working on a specific design you can add that from the drop-down here. Let's say you want to do this for an iPhone X screen size, it will create a canvas at the right size for that application. If that isn't enough you can also double-click on the Artboard Tool like you can most tools in Illustrator to access the Artboard options.

Artboard options

You may also access this from the Properties panel on the right by clicking this button, and once you've accessed the Artboard choices, you can rename the artboards. If you desire a specific size, you can select one of the defaults. You may enter the width and height parameters, your position in the workspace, and the orientation of the canvas, so if it's set up as a portrait and you need it to be landscape, you can change that as well. You have the option to constrain the proportions of the artboard as you resize it, and you have the display marks where you can show marks, show the cross hairs on the canvas, and show a video-safe area. You also have an option for "fade region outside of Artboard" and we'll show you what that does in a moment.

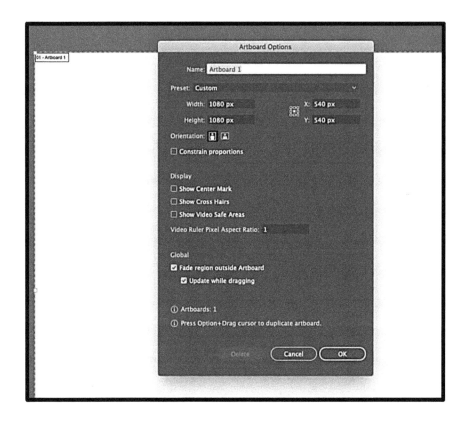

If we hit on it, it just brings up all those guides that we've just enabled through the Artboard options so the fade region is for when you are resizing and you'll see the faded area around the artboard as that's showing you the size of the new artboard. This means the faded region just allows you to see it as you're resizing the artboard.

Working with multiple Artboards

You now know how to work with a single artboard; however, you will need numerous artboards to work on a logo package, Instagram carousel, or something similar. If you need them to be the same size, pick the Artboard tool and then hold ALT or OPTION while dragging on the artboard to swiftly duplicate it. So, if you're working on a carousel and want to put them directly next to each other, and you have smart guides, you should be able to move the artboard into place and have it snap when it hits or meets the other artboard.

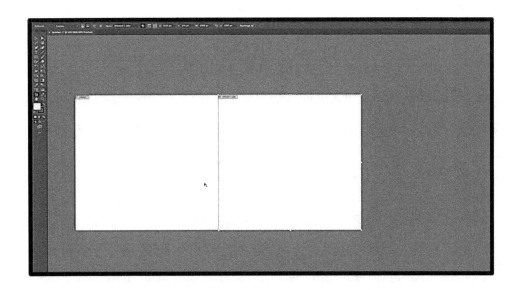

Creating a new Artboard

You can also make a new artboard by using the "New Artboard" button in the Control bar up there or the one on the right here.

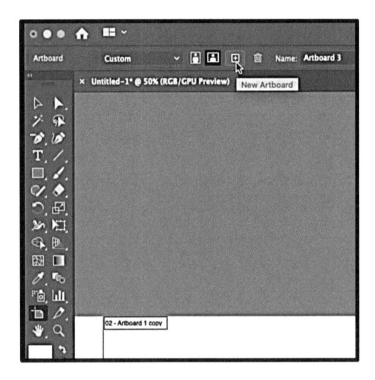

Resizing Artboards

Now you have multiple Artboards, let's say you want to resize them all to a different size - you can go through them manually and resize them all individually but you can also select each artboard, hold SHIFT as you're going through them, and select each one.

Rearranging Artboards

Any modifications you make to the width from the height up here will resize the artboards there, but you'll notice that they're all overlapping, which you can easily rectify. What you can do is select "Rearrange all" from the menu above, and from there, you can select the layout you want the artboards to follow, the columns you want the artboards to be in, and the space between them.

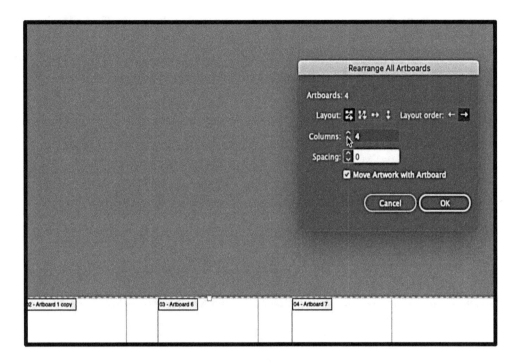

Let's say we want to establish the 0-pixel gap between the artboards and have them go left-to-right in a column of four. We'll enter all of that information and then hit OK. Now we can see that each of the previously prepared artboards is exactly positioned next to the other. This is useful if you're working on a project and the position of the artboards has gotten out of hand. It's also worth noting that it reorders based on the artboard number, so if you created them out of sync, they will remain out of sync, but you can fix this by going to the Artboard menu, which is accessible from the Window menu. Select Artboards and what this will do is it will bring up a list of all of the artboards in your document.

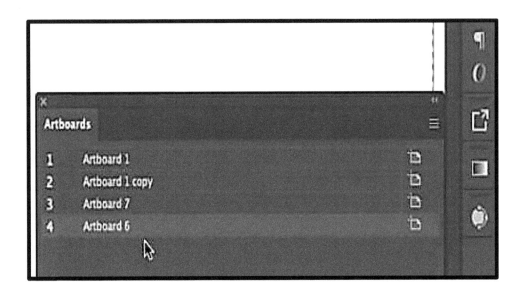

What you can do is rearrange the artboards in the order that you need them to be and how you want them to flow, but only if you rename them so you know which artboard is which. If you already know which artboard is which and the order that they need to go in, you can quickly and easily drag them into the correct order, then use the "Rearrange Artboards" option, which will reorder the artboards to the appropriate artboard number.

Converting a shape to an Artboard

What if we wish to use a form as an artboard? What if we're working in chaos and want a different size so we can add some art on top of it? What we can do is click on the Object menu, select **Artboards, and convert to Artboards**.

Now, the shape we chose is an artboard, so if you ever want to make your shapes or sizes, you can do so with the Rectangle Tool, and clicking will bring up a dialog box, so if we want an 8.5 x 11 piece of paper, we'll simply hit OK to confirm that. We can drop some art here, such as a tile, and if we want to export it, we can do so by clicking on the shape, which is 8.5 x 11 because it says so, and then going to Object, Artboards, and Convert to Artboard. The fun thing is we have all of this chaos but we can always come back here and click to reorder and this time we want it in three columns. We're going to hit OK and it's going to reorder all that artwork for us; it's going to move everything around and make it so that we can still work cohesively with all of these different artboards.

Exporting your Artboard

To export all of the Artboards that we've worked with at the same time we'll go to File, and then go to Export and then we're going to click on "Export for screens."

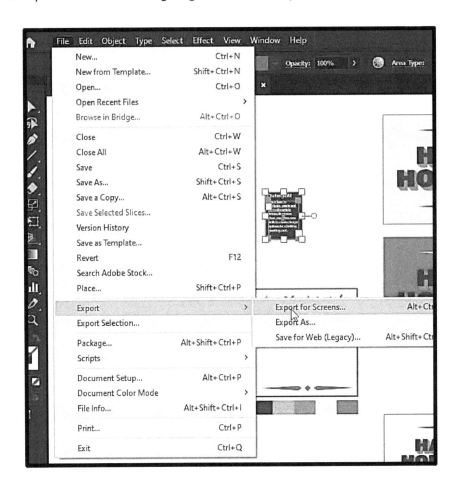

This is going to bring up a dialog box and when we're working with artboards we can usually do all of our naming here later. The options that we want are to include all we have and set it to go to the daily creative challenges folder.

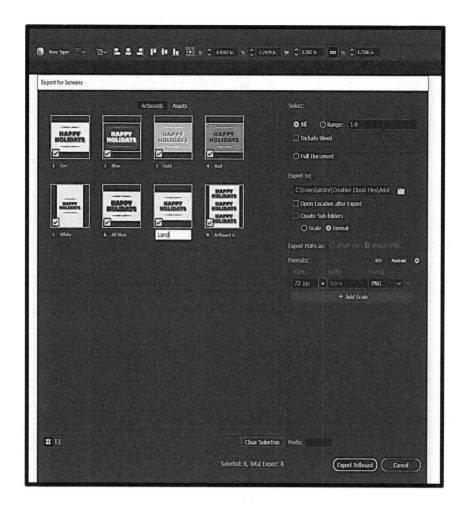

You can choose where you want yours to export to, and we don't want it to create subfolders because we're going to export numerous versions of this, so this is where things get exciting. We have 72 DPI for a PNG format, which we will preserve, but we will also add a scale. If we want to see a JPEG, we can click on JPEG 100, and it will make JPEG 100. You can enter any suffix and any type of name. You can also specify the scale; for example, if the jpegs are going to be printed, we want them to be 300 DPI because that is the norm for printing. We can specify that we want one more and that these be editable vectors, so we can select Add Scale, then SVG, which will export it as a vector.

We can put a prefix here if we like, and it will export as a challenge artboard. With the names, it will export these names because it is exporting each artboard and keeping its name. Finally, we'll select "Export Artboards." When we inspect the files, we can see that it produced a JPG, PNG, and SVG of each of our artboards, along with their names. We just exported a lot of different files without doing much, so as long as you name your artboards and keep them organized, you can go to File, Export, and Export for screens. Then you can fix up the names of your artboards and when you export everything will be named and sized in whatever you designate it to be right over here in this panel.

Review Questions

1. How do you make and change the size of artboards in Adobe Illustrator for different designs?
2. Why is it helpful to have multiple artboards, and how can you use them well in your design?
3. How can you move between artboards easily, and is there a way to share things between artboards in Adobe Illustrator?

CHAPTER 7

WORKING WITH LAYERS

In this chapter, we will discuss the Layers panel. The Layers panel is important because you will use it frequently in everything you do in Illustrator, so you should understand how to rearrange layers, rename layers, modify specific layers, and use various techniques with them, such as locking and hiding them, to see different aspects of your artwork. The Layers panel is useful for staying organized when you first start producing designs, especially if your designs have a lot of complicated elements or distinct aspects. You may only be creating one image or graphic, but when you get into something more complex, such as a poster design, and you have titles, sub-headers, body text, graphic images, background images, and textures, it can get confusing, and if it's all stuck on one layer, it makes it even more difficult, so we're going to show you how to create layers, navigate the Layers panel, and move things around.

Accessing the Layers panel

On the right side of your workspace is a little double square stack which is the symbol for your Layers panel. Click on that to open that up.

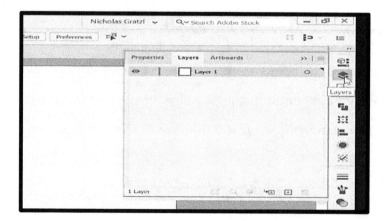

If you don't have it in your workspace, go to your Windows drop-down menu. It's right there. Click on that and this takes you right away to your layers panel and now you can see you've got some options here.

Deleting a layer

Down below, the first symbol is the trashcan and that's obviously to delete a layer so if you're done with it or if it's blank or you don't need that anymore you can go ahead and just delete that.

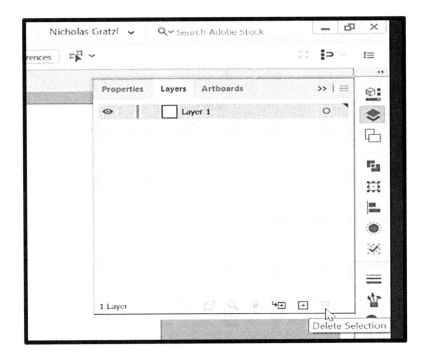

If you select remove and there's something in it that you're not aware of, such as a remnant, an Anchor Point, or an image, it will warn you and state there's an artwork in here, asking you to confirm if you want to remove it. This is a useful small feature in case you forget something.

Creating a new layer

The next little symbol, the square with the plus sign in it, that's how you create a new layer.
Click on that and you can see a new layer pops up.

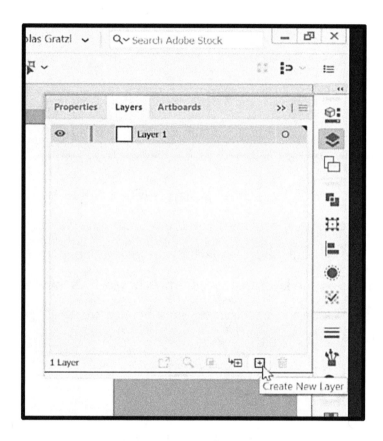

Creating a sub-layer

The next little symbol here creates a new sub-layer. So inside this layer, once you work on
layer one and let's say you create a new sub-layer and then draw a couple of shapes here,
you can see that layer has changed now. There's a little arrow symbol next to it.

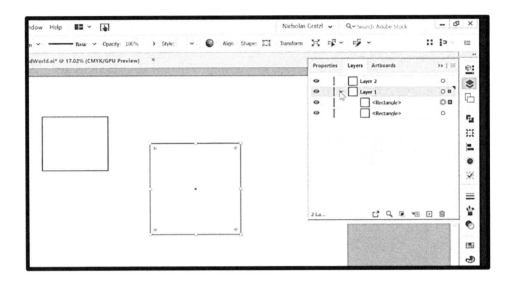

If you click on that arrow, it reveals the sub-layers within it, thus layer one contains two sub-layers, which are the two rectangles you drew. Every time you build something on a layer, it will be added as a sub-layer; this includes guides, a single Anchor Point, type, and anything else that is on the layer that is currently chosen. This implies that if you're on layer one, you can click on the small symbol right here to create a new sub-layer, and it will automatically place one within.

Creating a Clipping mask

The following functions may not be used frequently, but they allow you to make clipping masks. If you have a shape and an image overlaid on it, you can select the two and build a clipping mask of that shape or place that object inside that shape. That is a fantastic feature, but we'll teach you another way to apply clipping masks.

Exporting your layers

With the next two icons, you can collect all of your layers and export them as individual

layers, and then you can also locate objects in your design using that feature.

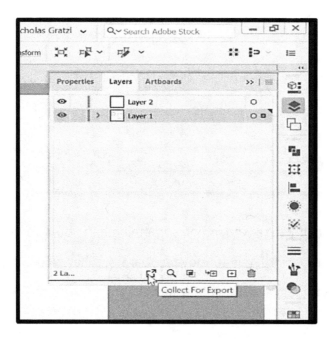

Hiding your layers and sublayers

Coming up to our Layers panel, we'd want to point out a few points. First, you have these small eyeballs, which are your visibility toggles. If you click on that, you can conceal whatever is in that layer, and if you open this arrow in your sub-layers, you can hide individual sublayers as well.

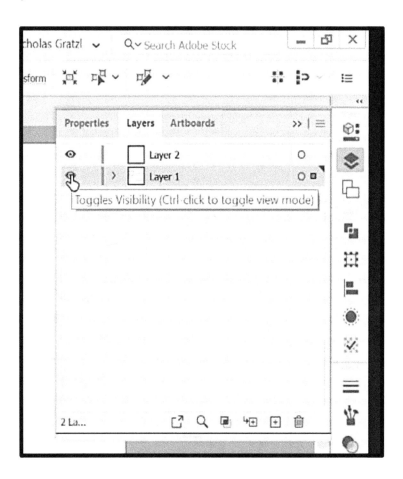

This is a great feature if you're working on something and you want to see what is behind that, how to get that behind, how to move forward or what would it look like if it wasn't here so that's great for just experimenting with different things or you just need to hide it for a moment.

Locking and unlocking your layers

Next, you'll notice a small blank square. If you click on that, it adds a lock, so when you hover over this square, you see that little pencil with the circle and a line through it, indicating that you can't do anything because the layer is locked.

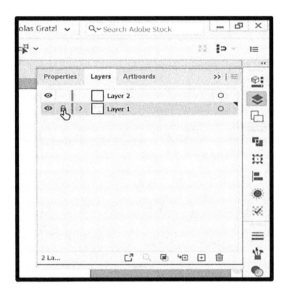

To unlock that just click on that lock icon and your square symbol comes up, you can now go to your Selection Tool, for instance, can click on any path and move that around or do what you want with it because it's unlocked.

Staying organized with Layers

Then you'll see the small colored bar. It's a nice little feature to help you find things, so right now everything in that layer will have a little blue color to it because it's in the layer with the blue box, and what's even nicer is that if you open up that layer, you'll see a little blue square pop up to let you know this is the sub-layer you're currently selecting, so if you select a shape in another sublayer, you'll see that shift.

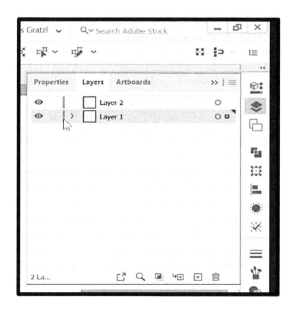

If you've got a layer with a ton of stuff in it and you're wondering where a particular shape or element is you can find it easily. It'll tell you what layer it's in out here and then if you click on the sub-layer it'll give you a slightly larger square and tell you the exact sub-layer so it's nice for finding things.

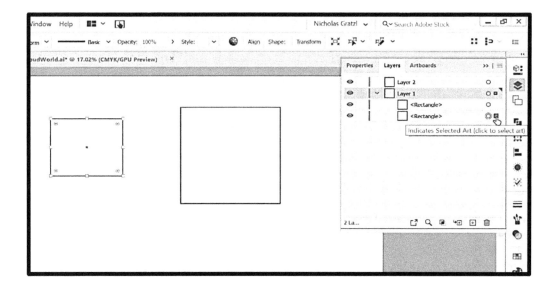

You want to try to stay organized when you get to more complex things since you've got a lot of things going on. Let's show you a quick illustration. We are going to go to Layer 2 and draw a circle or Ellipse here.

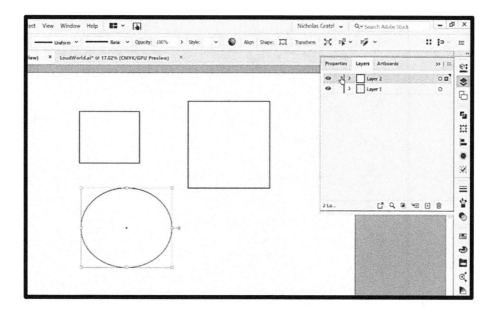

Since this layer is red, our bounding box and all of the features on that circle are also red. That's how it helps you keep track of those things, so if we click on that red bounding box, we can see that it now has an arrow because we have something in the layer, which implies there is a sub-layer that has the ellipse that we've chosen.

Renaming your layers

Double-clicking on the layer brings up the Layer Options window, where you can rename it. This is very useful if you're going through an iteration process or creating a logo and want to keep iterating it, so you might want to label some things or rename each layer.

Changing the color of your layer

You can also change the color of that layer. Let's say your layer is currently light red but you want to change that to green, you can do that using this feature.

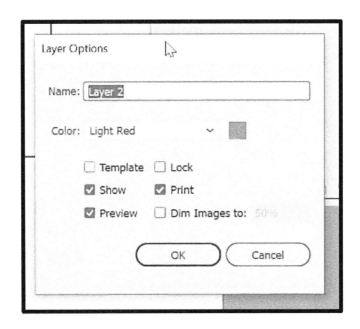

Creating a layer template

Another interesting feature we have here is the template option. You can use this when you bring a photograph into Illustrator. For example, if you bring in a photograph of yourself and want to create an illustrated self-portrait, you would create a new layer, place that image on that new layer, and then come in here and click the template, which dims the image 50% and automatically locks that layer. A simple explanation is to take a snapshot, cover it with tracing paper, and then lock it down. You can't do anything on that layer right now, so you can't draw on top of it, but if you add a new layer on top, you can start tracing and performing the work you need to accomplish. That's a handy feature if you want to trace a snapshot of something else because you can simply make a template and it'll lock it all in place for you.

Review Questions

1. Why do we use layers in Adobe Illustrator, and how do they help organize complicated artwork?

2. How can you create and organize layers in Adobe Illustrator to work efficiently?

3. Are there any special layer features in Adobe Illustrator that can help with editing or selecting specific parts of a design?

CHAPTER 8

WORKING WITH COLORS

Do you want to learn how to make stunning color palettes and locate the appropriate colors for your shadows and highlights when producing vector illustrations? In this chapter, we'll show you how to simply establish color palettes and how to draw and color your illustrations in Adobe Illustrator. There are two color modes: RGB and CMYK. What if you discover that your document is CMYK and you want to change it to RGB because the client has requested it, or if you unintentionally utilized the CMYK mode and now want to change it? We will show you exactly how to do this.

How to create custom palettes

We have here on our canvas a few color swatches. What we have is the lightest color we want to use in our illustration and the darkest but we need to find the colors that would go in between the mid-tones.

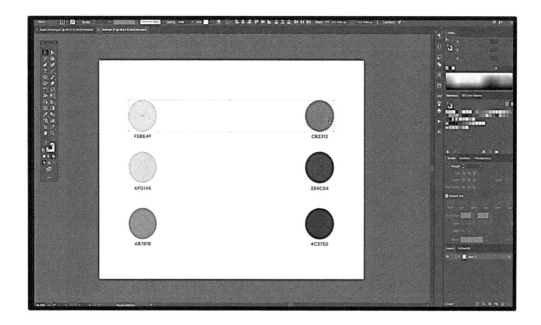

To do this, go to the top Object menu and pick "Blend." We'll go to the blending settings under **"Blend" and pick "Specified Steps"** from the drop-down menu. We'll alter the unit to three, giving us three mid-tones. Then we'll confirm by clicking **OK**, selecting the yellow color, and then selecting the red color using SHIFT. We will return to the Blend Tool and select "**Make.**"

This will automatically create the mid-tones between both colors. We'll do the same for the green and the brown.

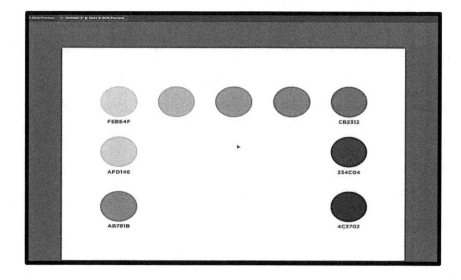

Now to turn these circles into actual shapes we'll head back to the Object menu, and select "Expand." With the object and fill selected, we'll click on OK.

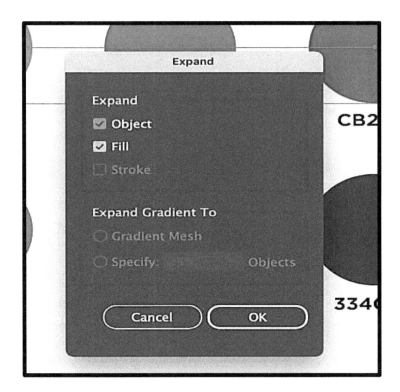

How to use the color palette

Now that we've generated the color palette, let's show you how to use it to color in illustrations. We'll outline the artwork with our simple Shapes and Pen Tool style first, and then apply the colors. First, select all and navigate to the Layers panel while holding OPTION or ALT on your keyboard. We'll drag the colored layer down to the other layer to make a duplicate, then lock and hide the outline layer. On the Color layer, we'll remove all small unneeded lines and details from the outline, then select and outline the stroke.

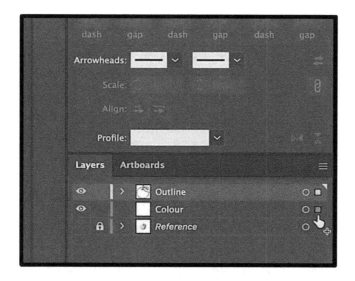

Head over to the Pathfinder panel and press the "Unite button" to merge all of your little

shapes. Now release the compound path and delete the outer top shape here.

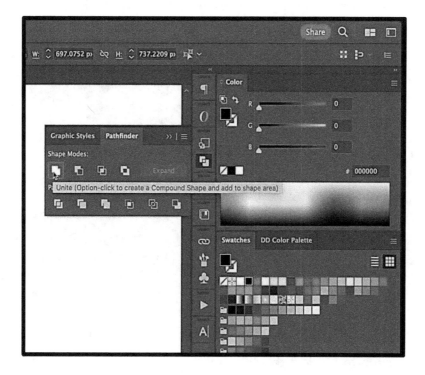

We're now ready to activate the outline layer, select each form, and add a mid-tone color to them. Using the darker colors, we may assign shadows to the bottom right of the artwork. We'll make sure you include some dark deep shadows, and for the highlights, we'll use a softer tone near the top left of the artwork. There you have it. This tutorial will show you how to use your color palettes to produce gorgeous, bright Vector graphics in Adobe Illustrator.

How to change color modes

In this section, let's take a look at how to switch between RGB and CMYK color modes. Firstly, when you start any new document in Illustrator by clicking the "New file" button or going to "File," and then selecting "New," in the dialog box at the bottom there's a Color mode selection. With this, you can select between RGB and CMYK.

Let's imagine we chose CMYK when we generated our project, or you've opened a new document and need to reselect the color mode. If we go to File or Edit, depending on whether you're on Mac or Windows, there's a document Color mode option right here. It displays it for you and allows you to select between CMYK and RGB. You may have some CMYK photographs or graphics in your document or something embedded, so you may receive a warning, but this is how you may switch between color modes.

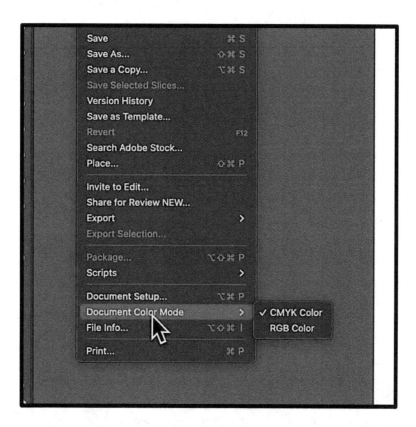

One other thing to show you here if we go up to Window, down to Color, our color out here could be displayed in a few different ways. This shows CMYK values but if we click the little hamburger menu we can switch what is shown and how we select our colors or pick our colors so we could switch it to RGB if that's what we want and now we have the HEX code down here and RGB values to work with.

So, if your color guides here are CMYK but you're in RGB mode, you can flip them right there. That's only an extra bit, and that's how you change color modes in Adobe Illustrator. After switching to RGB color, you will notice a shift in the gradient, which is due to some of the colors being recalculated. In RGB mode, the white light is noticeably sharper. If you want to see the color mode you are in, go to the document tab and look for the parenthesis.

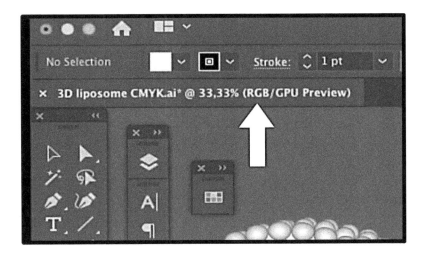

How to add a color swatch group

Are you looking for a quick approach to speed up your creative process? When saving color palettes in Adobe Illustrator, instead of adding each color individually as a new Swatch, which slows down the process, select all of your preferred colors, choose "**Add a new color group**," and then press **OK**, allowing you to access all of your colors in one spot.

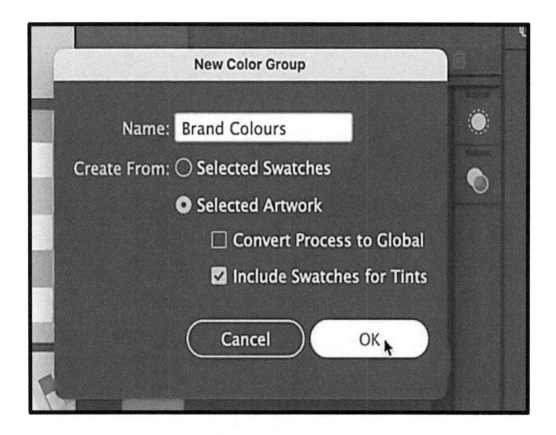

Review Questions

1. What are the different ways you can change the colors in Adobe Illustrator?

2. How do you make and save your own color choices in Adobe Illustrator so you can use them again?

3. Give examples of how picking the right colors can make your design look better.

CHAPTER 9

WORKING WITH TEXT

In this chapter, we will learn how to add and manipulate text in Adobe Illustrator. For this illustration, we obtained and opened a vector image in Illustrator. Before adding text to this image, we'll open the Character and Paragraph panels from the Window menu to quickly modify the font size, style, and alignment.

Entering your text

Click the Type Tool in the toolbar, then select the type of text you want to add. For a single line, simply click wherever in the document and start typing. For paragraph style, click and drag a text box within the document and begin typing. Drag the corners of your text box to resize it using the Selection Tool.

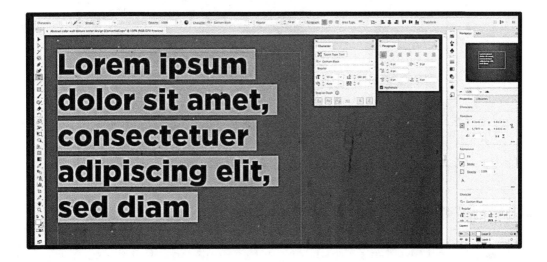

Repositioning your text

You can also reposition your text by dragging the object anywhere on your document. Once you've entered your text, use the Character and Paragraph panels to modify your font size, line spacing kerning, and alignment. You can select text and use the color picker to change its color.

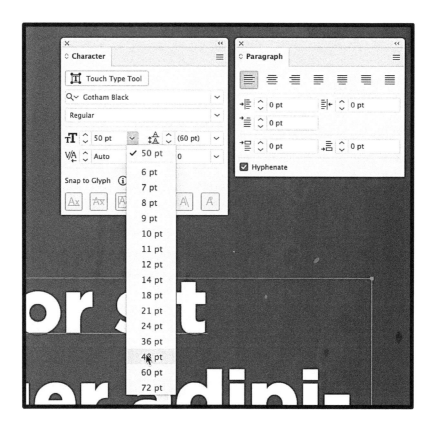

Adding text from your computer

A quick way to add text that's already on your computer in a text file such as a TXT or Microsoft Word file is to go to "File," "Place," then choose the text document from your computer and click "Place."

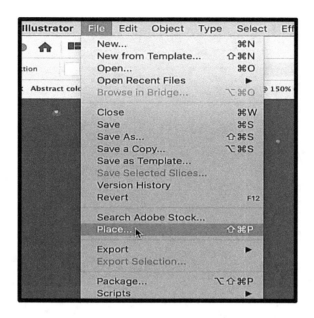

Make any necessary adjustments to the Options window, then click OK. Now, click and drag a Paragraph text box within the document; your text will be immediately inserted inside the box. If there isn't enough room in the box to display all of your text, a small red + box will appear in the bottom right corner, indicating that more information isn't being displayed.

Modifying your text

Now it's time to alter the wording. Let's imagine we wish to adjust the layout of our text so that it follows a path or curve. We'll begin by sketching a simple path with the Pen Tool, then reselect the Type Tool and hover near the left edge of the path. You will notice the cursor alter to signify text on a path. Click, and you'll be able to type right on your path.

The Direct Object Selection Tool allows you to change any point on your route, and the text will follow immediately. If we are unhappy with a character in a typeface or just want to change the appearance or restructure some characters, we can have Illustrator transform the text into editable objects. First, we'll add a line of text, then select "Type" and "Create outlines," and Illustrator will convert each letter into its shape. You can then use the Direct Selection Tool to change any of the points on any character.

Keep in mind that after you build an outline, Illustrator will automatically group all of your characters to keep their spacing consistent. To move individual characters more easily, simply select the text, then go to the Object menu and select "Ungroup." It's vital to note that after you've converted your text to outlines, it's no longer editable. Here's a little pro tip: converting text to outlines is also the best approach to ensure that your text always appears correctly when exported to any vector format. This is because Illustrator will not attempt to embed font files, some of which are incompatible and require the user to have the font installed on their machine within your project. Instead, your writing will be composed of standard vector shapes and objects. There's a lot you can do with text in Illustrator, and these are just a few quick and easy ways to get started.

How to Use the Retype Feature

In this section, we will look at the Retype tool in Adobe Illustrator 2024. For this illustration, we have a file with several prepared pictures, which are pixel images that we made, as well as a photo of the package, which is slightly deformed. We all know that's Lobster, but let's test if Illustrator recognizes it as well. Then we have our fonts utilized in these files, which are installed on the machine. We have an uninstalled Adobe typeface. In addition to Bickham Pro, we offer several OpenType features. Let's see what happens.

Now to enter it we are going to select the artwork, which is either a pixel image or an outline font. Then go to Type > Retype (beta).

You may also access this window from the Window menu, and Retype (beta) is down there, but let's go in and open it. We can see that it detects some writing here and even on the photo that is inside that image, and it sees all of the text and draws multiple dotted lines around it. That's because they're all in various fonts or are identified as distinct separate words.

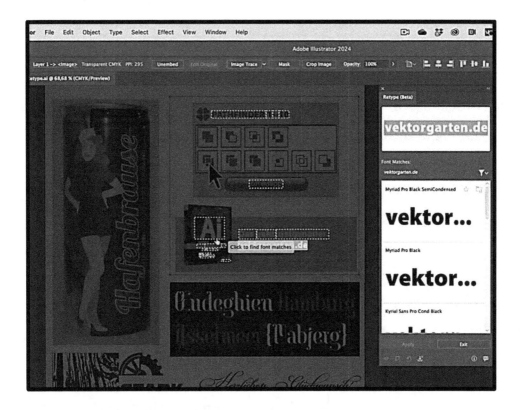

Now we can click on them to see which fonts Illustrator recognized, and if we don't think they match, we can look for more. This generates options that are sorted in the order in which they match best. In our case, we selected Myriad Pro because we didn't go far to build these, and Illustrator identified several similar ones that appear very close to Myriad.

If you want to have something extraordinary, you may just use it. We'll click on the one we want. We can double-click the text here to bring up the pop-up, which will inform us that

Illustrator wants to download some additional parts to this. Once the download is complete, the Retype functionality is ready to use.

Now we can double-click it, and after applying the font, it has changed this to live text, allowing us to depart and then edit it. Also, we should be able to select another one of them and get the appropriate font. Let us apply another Myriad one. Again, it has been changed to live text, so let us go in and do that as well.

After that, we'll check which one matches this. We're going to take anyone and apply, and we'll see what Illustrator comes up with. To verify this, we can see that Illustrator has even modified the photo and hidden the old pixel lettering. We'll go on to check out the others. With the panel open, we'll enter it, but it says text recognition failed because the text is deformed. This means that Illustrator recognizes some typefaces but not others for a variety of reasons. But now that you understand how it works, you can utilize it and have fun.

How to transform text prompt into Vector Graphics

Adobe Illustrator now includes a new "Text to Vector Graphic" function. In a new, empty document, you will not see "Text to Vector Graphic" in the contextual taskbar. Instead, you can access it using the "Properties" or "Text to Vector Graphic" panels. After using this feature once, it will appear in the contextual taskbar.

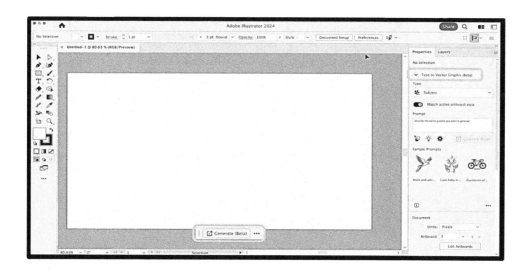

To access "Text to Vector Graphic", simply look for it in the Contextual bar, the Properties panel, or under the Window menu. By default, the output style will match the style of the active artboard. To change the setting toggle off the "Match active artboard style". Also, you can use the "Style Picker" to choose a style from an existing vector or image. Later, you can fine-tune your output level of detail from "Settings".

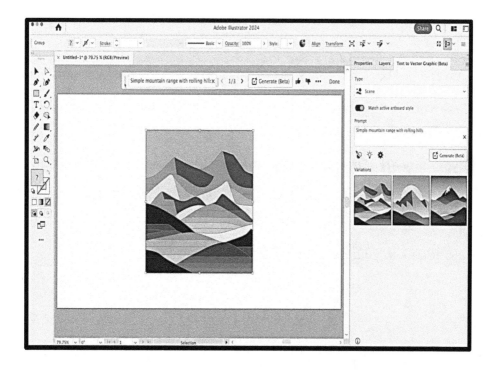

Now, let's generate a scene. Describe your vision and hit the "Generate" button. First-time users, make sure to agree to the user guidelines. Stay connected to the internet to avoid errors. Once connected, click "Generate" and you'll receive three variations. The first one is added to your artboard.

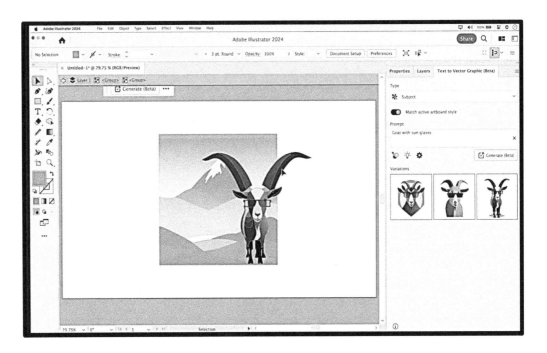

In the Contextual taskbar, use arrows to preview and select the one that suits your artwork best. Your generated vector graphic is neatly organized in groups for easy editing. Refine your selection with the Gradient tool or adjust the colors to your liking. Need to add a subject to your artwork? Draw a rectangle placeholder, then type in a description of the desired output in the prompt field and click "Generate." You can customize the color shapes, and size, as desired. You can also create icons effortlessly using this feature. It's versatile and adapts to your design needs.

Finally, let's explore "Text to Pattern". Type in a description of the desired output in the prompt field and click "Generate." Ensure your instructions are accurate; any spelling mistakes can lead to errors. We've already created a path using the Pen Tool, meticulously outlining the sofa seating cushion. Now, let's add a pattern from the generated variations.

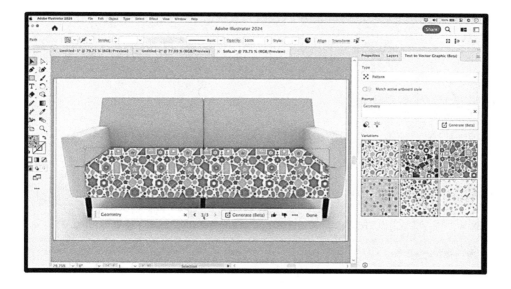

To enhance the outcome further, let's play with blend modes. Go to the Transparency panel. Here, add a blend mode; for instance, we chose "Multiply" and this beautifully blends all the textures and shadows, just like it would in real life. These options allow you to incorporate details from the raster image, such as lighting effects, curves, and distortions. Explore the "Presets" and "Color controls" to refine and limit your output colors.

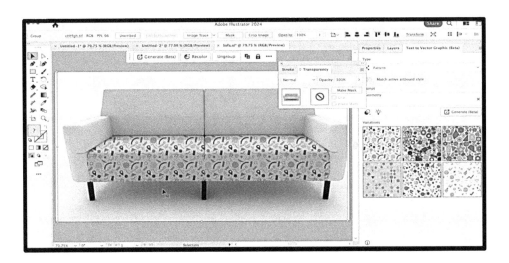

You can even incorporate your brand's color palette using this. With endless possibilities and use cases, we can't wait to see what you create.

Review Questions

1. How do you add text to your design in Adobe Illustrator?

2. Explain how to make the text look shadowy or have a cool-colored background in Adobe Illustrator.

3. How can you change the text appearance without losing the ability to change their size or look?

CHAPTER 10

HOW TO EDIT ILLUSTRATOR TEMPLATE

In this chapter, we are going to show you how to edit Illustrator templates like replace images, color change, and make a file ready for printing.

How to replace images

If you want to replace images then you need to open the Link panel. Go to Window then click on the "Link" option.

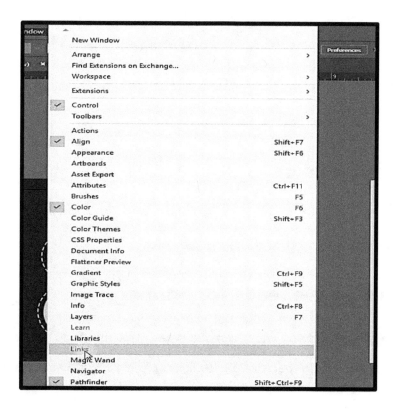

First, select the Direct Selection Tool, click on the image then go to the Link option and click on "Relink."

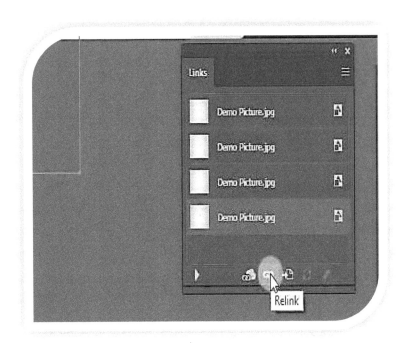

Now select the image and click on "Place."

How to change color

If you want to change color then select all objects using CTRL+A. When all objects are selected go to Recolor Artwork and change the color.

How to make a file ready for printing

When your file is okay and you want to make it ready for printing then you need to save the file as pdf format. To do that, go to File click on "Save as" and select Adobe PDF.

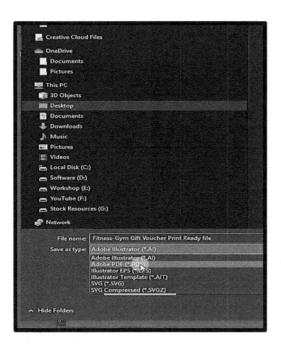

Now select high-quality print, click on "Marks and Bleeds" as checking the trim marks and bleed is most important for printing, then click on Save.

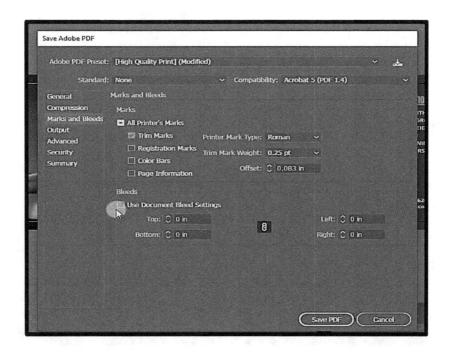

How to open a template

Open your Adobe Illustrator; you can see the Menu and Tools panel. Now go to the File menu, click on Open, and select your template. This will open your file in the illustrator.

How to edit text

If you want to replace or edit a particular text then go ahead and open the Character panel. Go to the window and click on "**Character**." Now select the Type Tool, make a selection of the text, and type or paste it here. You can control the text size and style from the Character panel.

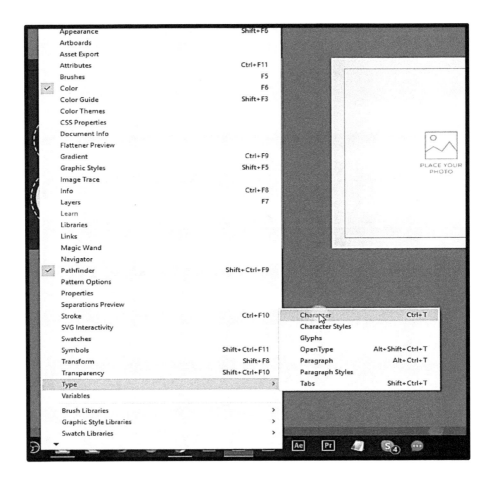

Review Questions

1. How do you change an already-made Illustrator design to fit what you want, like changing the colors or moving things around?

2. Are there any important tips to keep in mind when changing Illustrator designs to make sure everything looks good together?

3. How can you make an Illustrator design template look like it's yours?

CHAPTER 11

WORKING WITH GRADIENTS, PATTERNS AND BLENDS

This chapter takes you into more advanced work in Adobe Illustrator. Here, we will cover topics like how to easily use the gradient tool and create gradients like a pro, create beautiful patterns, and utilize the blend tool.

Understanding gradients

In this section, we are going to show you the three ways you can create gradients in Illustrator by showing you these three famous app icons (Facebook, Tinder, and Instagram) as examples.

Linear gradient

Let's begin by showing you how to use the linear gradient. The Facebook logo we have here has a vertical gradient going from light to dark blue so for this illustration, we will copy it, select the gray area here, and head over to the Gradient panel.

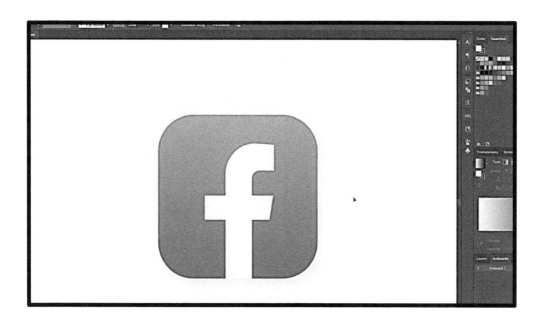

We will click on the first option which is the linear gradient and this will assign the logo a default white-to-black gradient transition.

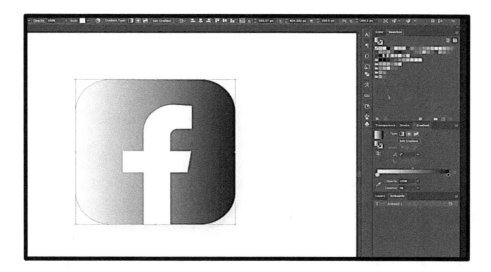

Let's now apply the custom colors to it by going into the Color palette. We will select a light blue and just drag it on top of the white dot on the Gradient panel. We will do the same for the dark blue and this will apply the correct colors to the logo.

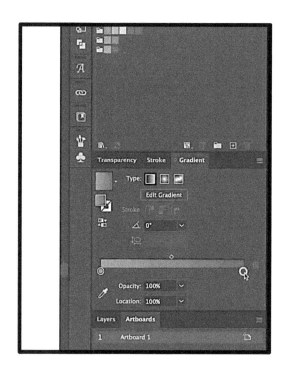

Now the example here has the color transition going horizontally so let's change that. We are going to press the letter G on our keyboard to activate the Gradient Tool then just click at the top, hold SHIFT on our keyboard, and drag down the gradient, and simply enough, we have created a linear gradient.

Radial gradient

The radial gradient is just as easy as the linear one. This gradient has its color transition starting from the center outwards. For example, we have the Tinder logo which we are using for this illustration. We can see the subtle transition from orange to pink.

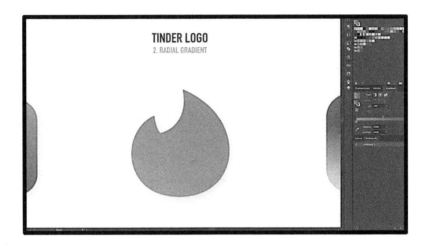

Let's select the example here, head over to the Gradient panel, and click on the Radial option. From the panel, we are going to apply the orange color to the left side and the pink color to the right side. Then we'll select the Tinder logo and activate the Gradient Tool by pressing G on our keyboard.

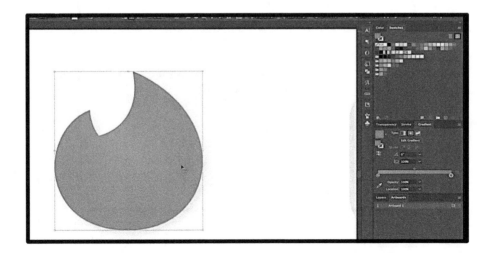

Once again, we'll click towards the bottom left and drag out the gradient upwards and there we have it.

Freeform gradient

Lastly for this section, we're going to show you how Instagram created this beautifully colored logo with the freeform gradient. As you can see there are more than two color transitions and they all start from different areas but then, let's show you how to do this.

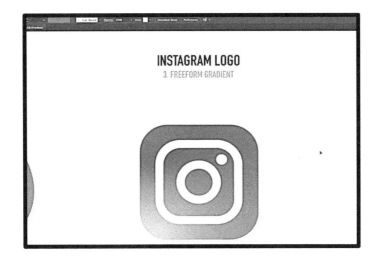

First, click on the gray logo head over to the Gradient panel, and select the third option which is the freeform gradient. As you can see here the circle will appear over the shape. We can assign a color to it or even add multiple circles.

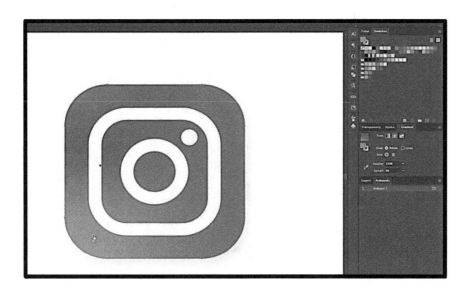

Let's begin by placing the circle at the top left and assign a blue color to it then, just assign colors from the color palette where you see fit to copy the Instagram logo. To add more circles all you have to do is click elsewhere and there you have it.

Using the Gradient tool

If you have the Gradient Tool selected you can also add a type of gradient. We have three types: linear-gradient, radial gradient, and freeform gradient. Linear gradient is easy - it's going to go from one to the other and with the Gradient Tool you can select where that starts and stops. Now with this Gradient Tool selected if you look at the line drawn across here in the middle we have a beginning color and an end color. The gradient itself goes between the furthest colors so if we bring white in, the gradient only starts where this color exists after that it's all pure white same with the black, you can tell after this black it's all just that swatch so if we bring this out, our gradient is going to run from one end to the other.

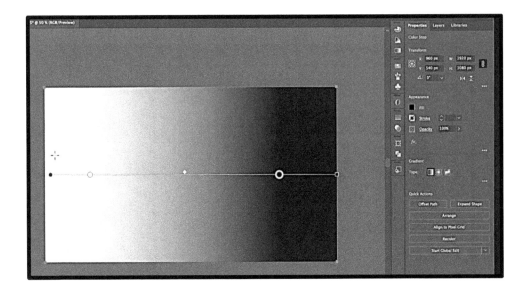

The little black dots allow you to adjust where the edges of the bounds of that gradient are. The one on the left moves it and the one on the right allows you to scale in and out, and you can always redraw that gradient if you want to. The diamond in the middle is basically which color has more influence on this gradient so it starts to transition a little slower until it hits this diamond and then it translates a little quicker to black or vice versa. The other thing you can do is Click the three dots under the Properties panel and you can see your gradient right here. You can add colors to it. Simply double-click on that gray and change it to a color of your choice. You can also change the colors here by going over to these color swatches and double-clicking on them which opens up your Swatches panel or the Palette or a Color Picker.

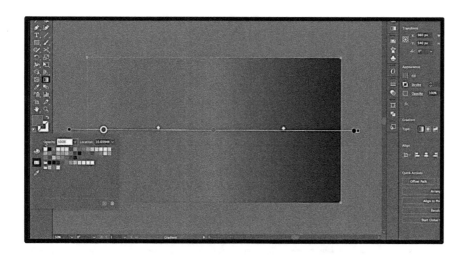

Adding transparency to your gradient

If you want to color-pick the gray color out here you can do that by selecting the color of your choice. You can even adjust the opacity as well so what if you want to go from red to the same red but you want the red on the left to be more transparent you can just double-click on that and change the opacity to zero and press return or click outside of that box.

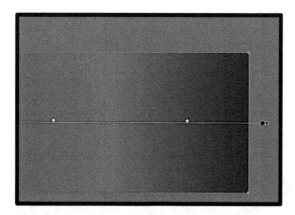

Now it looks like white but if you click and drag the shape up you'll notice that it's not white and that you're seeing white because your background color is white, meaning it's transparent. So no matter what color is underneath it you can see it a little bit better with the gray and you can see it when it overlaps here, how it goes from red to transparent.

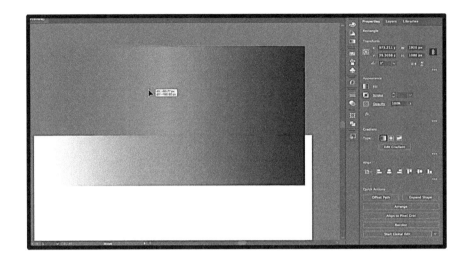

Manipulating your Gradient

If you want to get back to edit this gradient make sure the Fill is selected. You can grab the Gradient Tool and everything pops up again or you can see the Gradient feature over here in the Properties panel and adjust the gradient here with these three dots. You can change the angle of your gradient and that adjusts depending on where you draw it. You can remove a Swatch just by clicking and dragging it a little bit further down. You can also click on it and click the trash can to remove the Swatch as well.

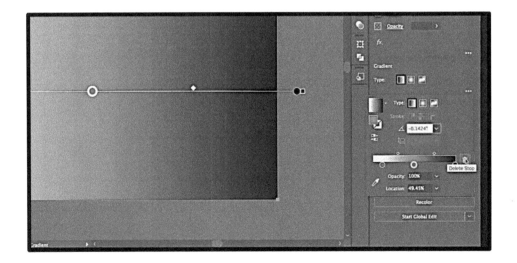

137

This gradient can be applied to a stroke or fill if you want it. You can also have the gradient Swatch but if you increase that stroke weight to something a lot larger like 50 you can see how that gradient applies to the stroke. Now because you switched those swatches you could apply it to both if you wanted to just by clicking and dragging so there's a gradient on the fill and a gradient on the stroke.

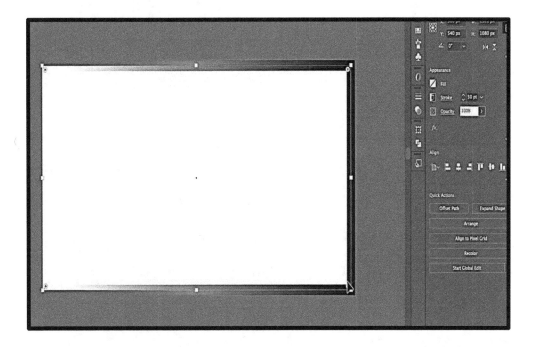

You might have to make some adjustments here if you want them to be the same as each other or you would just include the gradient on one or the other, in this case, we're going to look at gradients on the fills so we're pressing G for our Gradient Tool again and now that you know all the basics we can switch this gradient to a radial gradient. Radial gradients are going to start from the center out in a circular pattern.

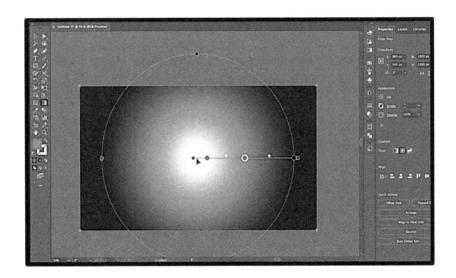

The last gradient we have to talk about is a new one called the freeform gradient. We also call it a Mesh gradient. What it does is it adds points out here that are like their own little radial gradients with a blur.

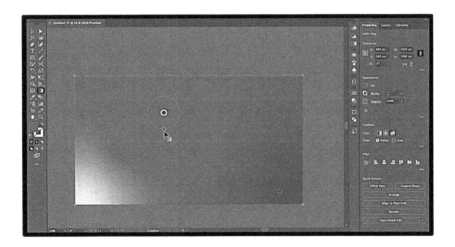

You can adjust the intensity of each of these points so you can have multiple gradient spots and you can see you have a little plus icon which means you can click and add another point. You can also change the color of those points by double-clicking on them and grabbing a different color from your swatches. You can move these points around to wherever you want these gradients to apply, you can click and drag their intensity which is how much these influence the other points. Bring them closer to each other and they'll all just blend. It's a cool way to create gradients here with this Freeform Gradient Tool.

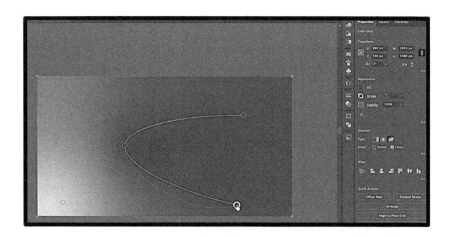

Our gradient tool defaults to just adding points but you can add lines and what that means is from one point or one gradient Swatch to another you could add a line and that's going to create some definite interesting effects here within your Freeform gradient. Press the ESC key to stop that line and then you can change how these gradient points affect what's going on and how the different points blend here in your gradient. It's a really interesting way to add different effects here to the gradient. Another thing here is that you can change the opacity of the different points as well to show a little bit of the background.

How to make a gradient blend

In this section, we are going to show you two ways of making multi-color gradient blends that you might not have thought of before.

Method 1

First, we're going to do a gradient blend, and this will take two different gradients and blend them. On one side, we're going to have an orange and a pink gradient, and on the other side, we'll have a purple-to-yellow gradient. To do that, we're just going to get on our Gradient Tool and also bring up our Gradient panel over here. Now, if you're not seeing the Gradient panel, you can come up under Window, and it'll be under there.

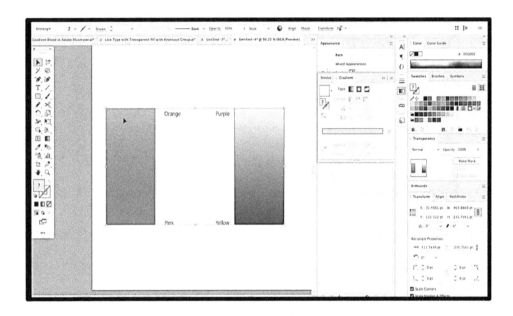

Next, we're going to click right here on the Gradient to give us a white and black gradient then we'll double-click here to set our color. Going into our palette, we are just going to choose, we'll go with orange, then click our pink and another color. We'll change it to 90 degrees. So now we have our orange-to-pink gradient. We are getting back on our Selection Tool because we don't want a stroke, so we'll bring that to the front and then just get rid of it. Now, since the first one is already set up, we're going to delete it and just make a copy of the second one, holding SHIFT and OPTION or ALT and dragging. We'll get back on our Gradient Tool, and then just change the colors to purple and yellow. You can also do that right here in the Properties panel. Now we'll select both of these and blend them. To do that, we're going to come here to the Object menu and go to Blend and Blend Options.

141

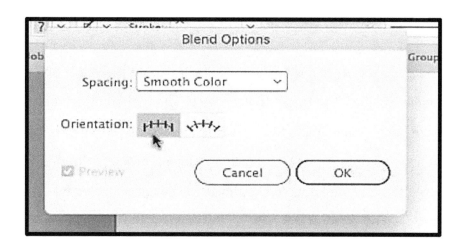

We just want this to be Smooth color, and it doesn't matter the orientation on this since it's two squares, and then we'll say OK. Sometimes your smooth gradients work, at other times they seem inconsistent. So if we want a smooth-looking gradient, all we have to do is go to the Object menu, select "Blend and Blend Options," change this to "Specified steps," and we can make this about a hundred, and we'll say OK. Then we'll go over to Object > Blend and Make. You can also hit SHIFT + COMMAND + B or SHIFT + CTRL + B on a PC. And now we have the beautiful gradient that we are expecting. So that's the first way of making the multi-color gradient.

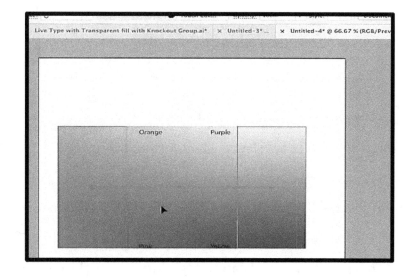

Method 2

The second way you can try is the freeform gradient, and to make this one, you can just make a rectangle. Simply hit M to get to your Rectangle tool and then draw a box. Next, in your Gradient panel, you're going to choose the very last option which is called freeform gradient and now it automatically starts with a gradient, giving us four nodes. Now, the cool thing about this is we can double-click these to change our color; we can move them around so they take up more of the area, and we can even click down here and expand the gradient that way. We are going to make this gradient look pretty similar to the first one. We'll make that orange, and then double-click the first one to make it yellow. We'll include a darker purple and pink.

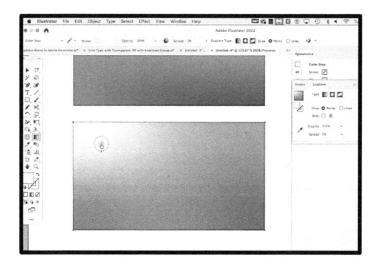

Now we have two very similar multi-color gradients, but they're just made differently. One cool thing to do with these is to overlay white text as this gives it a nice effect. Also, because these are made differently when we expand them, we get two different results. Let's go to Object > Expand Appearance to show you what we mean, and then we'll do Object > Expand. We'll expand the object and fill, and we have the option to change this to a gradient mesh but we'll just go ahead and tell it to do 255 objects, and we'll say OK.

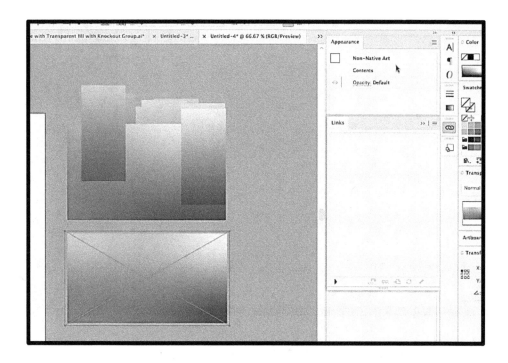

Normally when you expand a gradient, you get a lot of little pieces. You can hit COMMAND+Y or CTRL+Y to toggle in and out of Outline mode so you can see the difference here. If we use our Group Selection Tool, all of these are different pieces. And now, this one has been changed to something called non-native art; it changes it to an image, and just like all gradients, this may cause printing problems, so just be aware of that.

Create Editable Gradient Text

In this section, you will learn how to create editable gradient text in Illustrator. Type in some random text, then scale this up and change the font if you want. Now if you apply a gradient to this text nothing will happen, even though Illustrator might be showing that there is a gradient. What you have to do is just cancel out the gradient and you'll see that the text is there but it's invisible. Now go to the Appearance panel and add a new fill.

144

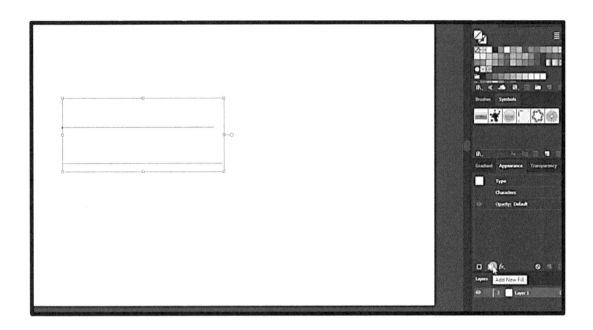

What it will do is change the color of the text to black and now you can go to gradient and just click on it. After that, you can apply some colors; if you change the text you will see that the gradient is applied to this text as well.

Working with patterns

Have you ever wondered how patterns work in Illustrator and how you can create one? If your answer is yes then you're in the right place. In this section, you will learn all that you need to know about patterns in Adobe Illustrator.

Accessing your in-built Patterns

Before you start to design your patterns you should know that Illustrator comes with a nice set of patterns that can be easily accessed from the Swatches panel. If the Swatches panel is not opened you can easily do it by going to Window in the menu bar and selecting Swatches. To get access to your built-in patterns all you have to do is click the Swatches button, go to Patterns and here you will find the lists of patterns that come with Illustrator.

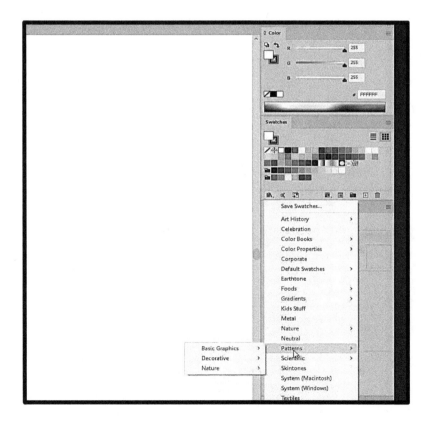

Select one and Illustrator will open a new panel where you can visualize and select the desired pattern. Keep in mind that by using these arrow buttons you can easily navigate to the next or the previous pattern collection.

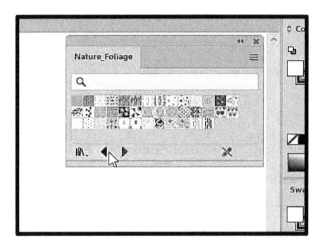

To use one of these patterns, you need to first select it which will add it to your Fill. If you select one of these vector shape tools it creates a new shape that will be filled with your selected pattern.

Adding patterns to shapes

To add a pattern to an existing shape you need to select that shape and then click the pattern that you wish to apply for the fill or even for the stroke. You can see every new pattern that you apply gets added inside the Swatches panel which makes it easier to use it again.

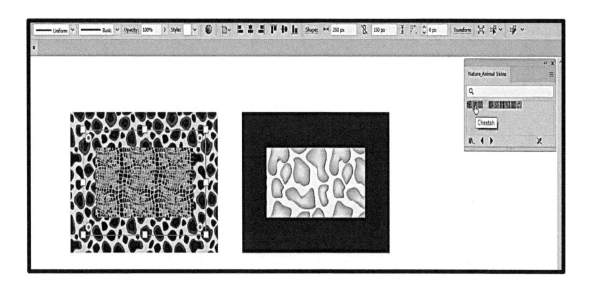

Applying a pattern to a text

Applying a pattern to a piece of text can be just as easy. Select the Type Tool from your toolbar and type in your new text or select a piece of text that you already have. Make sure that you have the "Fill" selected then click the pattern that you wish to apply.

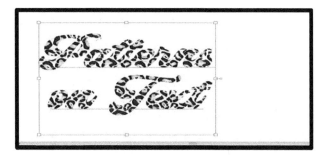

Creating your custom pattern

These built-in patterns can be really useful but in some cases, you might have to create your own pattern. Illustrator comes with a dedicated Pattern-building tool in the form of the Pattern options panel. You can easily open this panel by heading over to Window and

"Pattern options" and by default your panel should be inactive. To use all the functions from this panel you have to select the artwork that you wish to turn into a pattern.

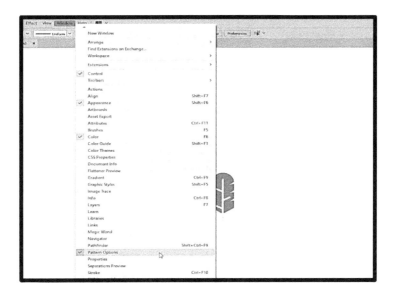

Open the pattern menu and go to "Make pattern." This will save your pattern inside the Swatches panel and bring up editing mode. In this mode, you have access to all the settings from the Pattern options panel and a live preview of your pattern. The original tile keeps the full opacity while the copies are a bit dimmed.

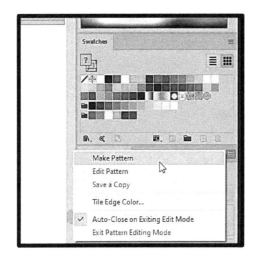

Editing your pattern

Now that your pattern is saved let's have a closer look at this Pattern panel and see how you can edit your pattern.

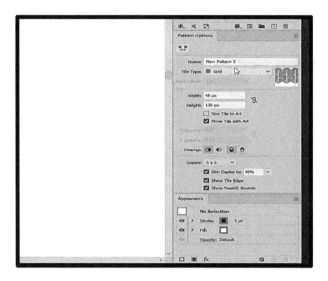

In the name box, you can type in a name for your pattern. From the File Type drop-down menu, you will decide the tile type and how the tiles should repeat. When you choose Grid, Brick by Row, or Brick by Column, your tiles are treated as being rectangular while when you choose Hex by Column or Hex by Row, your tiles are fitted as being hexagonal.

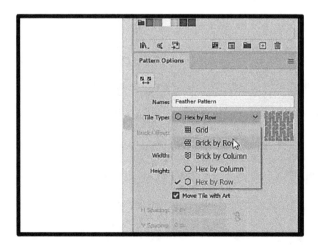

Selecting the Brick by Row File Type will give you access to the Brick Offset function. This setting lets you offset your tiles and you can choose between eight different values which produce different results. If you wish to scale your tile you can do it by adjusting the values from the Width and Height boxes or by clicking the square button which will activate a bounding box around your tile and now you can manually adjust your tile.

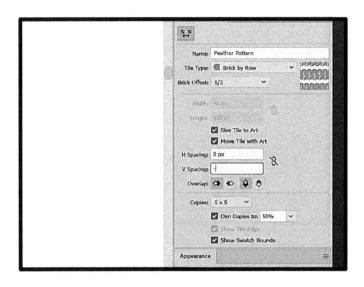

Whenever you increase the size of the tile beyond that of the artwork, Illustrator adds space which will increase the spacing between tiles. When you decrease the values, the tiles end up overlapping. To remove any unwanted overlapping returns to the original size values. All you have to do is check the "Size tile to art" box. The other box ensures that moving the artwork will make the tile move as well. Whenever you have the first box checked you can adjust the spacing between your tiles using these two values. Entering negative values will make your tiles overlap which takes us to these next settings that let you decide which tiles should appear in front when your tiles overlap. Moving to the bottom of this panel, the "Copies" settings can be used to set the look of your pattern preview. From this menu you can select the number of copies that should make up your pattern preview, you can increase or decrease the opacity of these copies or completely

151

disable the dim effect. Finally, with the two boxes below that, you can turn on and off the visibility for the tile edge or the Swatch bounce. The Swatch bounce displays the portion of the artwork that needs to be repeated to create the actual pattern design. It might help you to better understand how patterns work as it allows you to see exactly where your shapes need to be for the tile transition to appear seamless. When you're done editing your pattern make sure that you click the "Done" button to leave editing mode and then you can use one of the Vector Shape tools to create a new shape that's filled with your pattern.

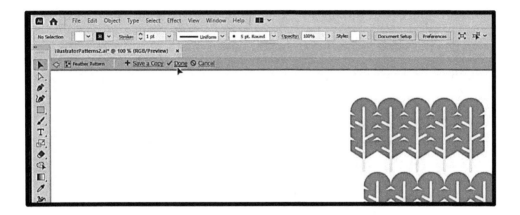

Creating your pattern from scratch

Now that you're familiar with the basic pattern-building techniques let's see how you can create your wave pattern from scratch. Start by selecting the Ellipse Tool from your toolbar. Click on your artboard to create a 66-pixel circle, remove the stroke color, and select Fill. Change the color to 71, 87, and 94, and then go to Object, "Path and offset path." Set the Offset to -4 pixels. Click OK to create the new shape, change the color to 88, 239, and 255, and go again to Object, Path, and Offset path, but keep the offset at -4 pixels. Click ok to create the new shape.

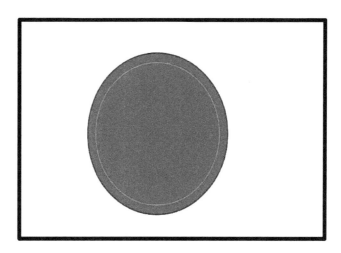

Grab the Eyedropper Tool from your toolbar and use it to fill this new shape with a color. Continue to use the same technique until you get to the center of the circle. Go again to Object > Path and Offset path, and keep the offset at -4 pixels. Click OK and fill the new shape with this color.

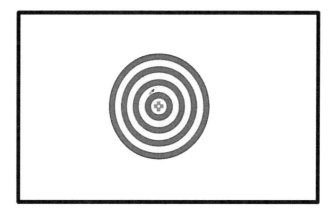

Now switch to the Move Tool so you can select all these circles that will serve as your pattern tile. Go to Object > Pattern > Make, to save these shapes as a new pattern and open the Pattern options panel where you can set the settings of your pattern.

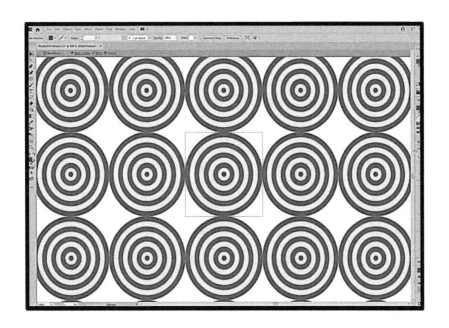

You can name it Wave pattern. Select Brick by Row for the tile type, lower the width to 62, the height to 30 pixels, and keep the rest of the settings as they are. If you wish, you can play with the "Overlap" settings to adjust the direction of your pattern. Once you are done, click the "Done" button to save the settings for this new pattern. Select one of these Vector Shape Tools then create a new shape and fill it with your new pattern.

Scaling your patterns

Once applied, you might want to scale your pattern and if you try the classic method you might notice that the pattern does not scale. This happens because of a setting from the general menu that you can easily enable or disable by going to Edit > Preferences > General. Check the "Transform pattern tiles" option then click OK and now if you try to scale your shape you can see that your pattern scales with the shape.

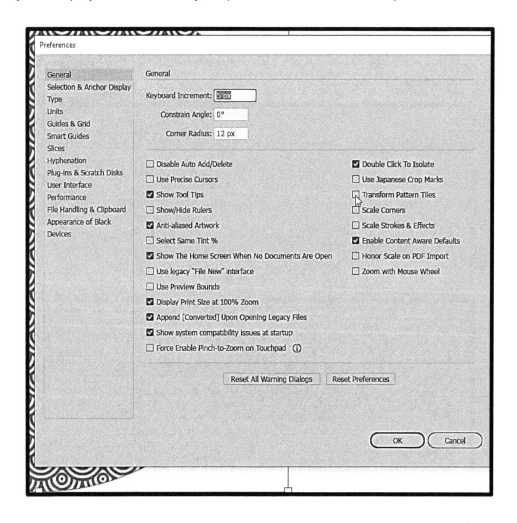

Another method that can be used to scale an applied pattern is to go to Object > Transform > Scale. Make sure that you uncheck the "Transform Objects" box so that the pattern will scale and not the entire object and then you can play with the horizontal and vertical values to scale the pattern or you can check the "Non-uniform" box if you are looking for a non-uniform scaling.

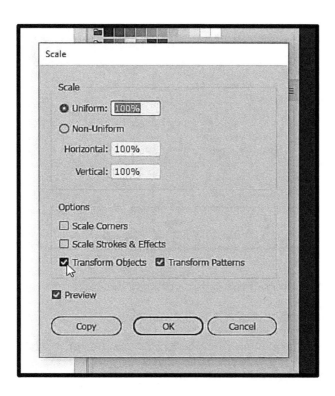

The third method that can be used to scale or even rotate an applied pattern is to go to Effect > Distort and transform > Transform. Play with these sliders to scale your pattern. Make sure that you enter identical values if you are looking for a uniform scaling. Again, uncheck the "Transform Objects" box to scale the pattern and not the entire object and you can play with that Angle spinner to rotate the pattern as you wish. Click OK to apply this effect.

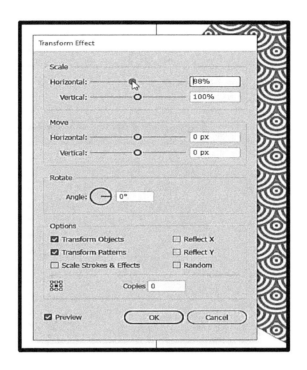

The nice thing about this technique is that you can always return to the Appearance panel where you can find this effect, open it, make some new changes, Click OK and the changes will be applied in an instant. Now that you know how patterns work feel free to use your imagination and create your pattern designs.

Making blends

In this section, we're looking at using the Blender Tool in Illustrator. For this illustration, we are going to select a color to use then we're going to make a shape. It doesn't matter what shape you make, the shapes that you use for the Blend Tool can be the same or they can be different. Having made this one shape we are going to make a star and we'll give it a different color because then you'll see the full power of the Blend Tool as we work. Now we have a star that is roughly in alignment with the square.

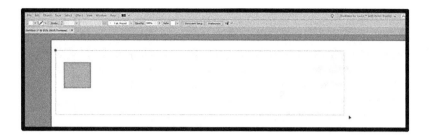

The Blend Tool

To use the Blend Tool you're going to select your shapes then go to Object > Blend > Make, and this makes a blend between the two shapes. What you see here may not be exactly what we see, it depends on whether you've used the Blend Tool previously or not because you might have it set to something different.

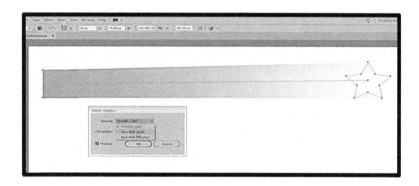

To see the settings select the blend, go to the Blend Tool, and click on it once to open the Blend options dialog. You'll need to turn on the preview so you can see what you're doing at the moment. We've got a Smooth color and a smooth transition. This has gone smoothly from the first color to the second color. We've also transitioned from being a square to a star. We are now going to select "Specified steps" from this drop-down list and wind our steps back to say 6 because then it's going to be clear what's happening here.

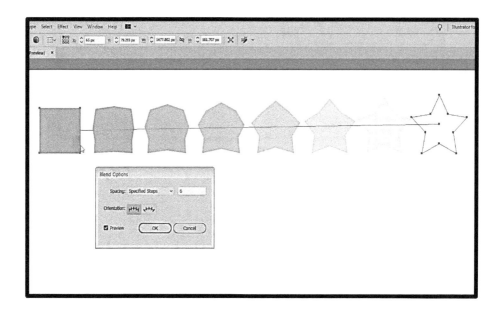

What Illustrator is doing is blending these shapes into each other; it's sort of morphing them as it goes so it's morphing the shape as well as the color. The next step is something else that you need. To be able to get these shapes out of the blend you're going to have to expand it. If we look here in the Layers palette we can see that we've got a bind in the Layers palette and the actual shapes aren't shapes yet we've got a star and the square and we've got the path along which the star and square are being blended. If we want these individual shapes we have to do something about that and that is to expand our blend.

Expand your blends

To do that we are going to choose Object > Blend, then go down to "Expand" and that just expands the blend into the individual shapes so we end up with one shape for each of these objects.

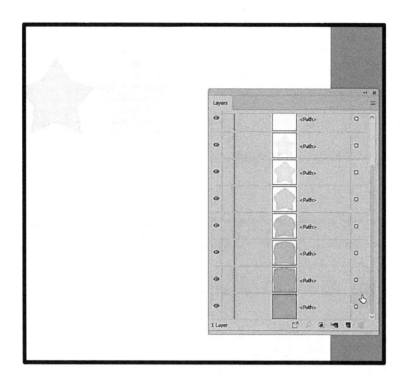

Blend around a shape.

Moving forward, we are now going to show you how you can blend around a shape. We're going to start again with our star shape but let's make it a different color this time. We'll make it a sort of pink and drag out a small star. For our second object, we are just going to blend from one star to the other so we're going to settle for two pink stars.

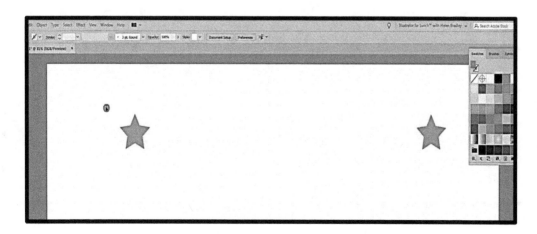

160

We'll select them, go to Object > Blend > Make. This time things aren't joining up the same way that they did last time. With our blend selected, we'll go back to the Blend Tool, and double-click on it to get the blend options. It's set to smooth color, we can do specified steps and if we take up the number of steps we can see how they blend into each other. This would probably be more apparent if we were transitioning from say a pink star to a blue star.

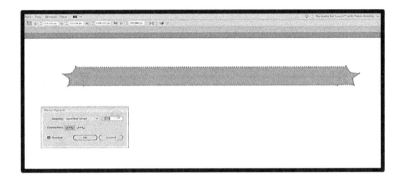

We are just going to reduce the number of steps that we've got on our blend so let's just take it down to 6. It's important to note that when you have specified 6 steps you're going to have eight stars so we've got one on either end and six in the middle. We are just going to click OK.

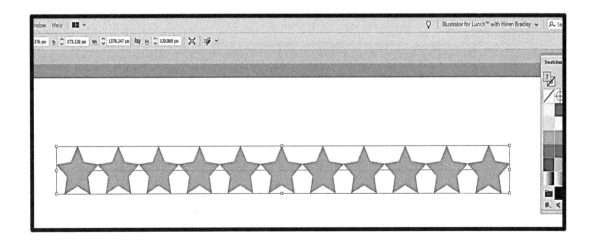

Now we want to put these stars around a circle and the way we do that is to draw our circle using the Ellipse Tool and we're just going to drag out a circle by holding the SHIFT key as we do that so that we are making a perfect circle for this.

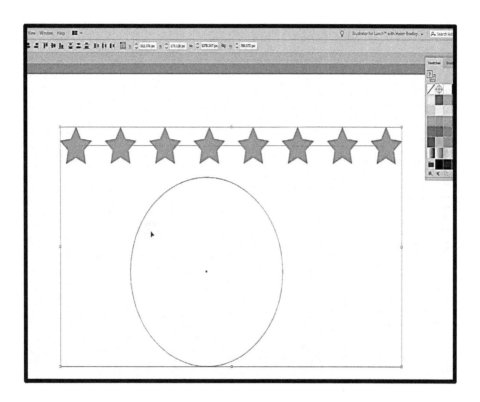

We can now go and apply the color as a stroke rather than a fill (it doesn't matter, we don't need a stroke or anything in this circle, we just need the circle to be made), then we're going to select both the blend and the circle. It doesn't matter what order they were created in, Illustrator is going to recognize which ones are Blend and which ones are circles. We're going to place the stars around the circle by going to Object > Blend and doing something called "Replacing spine."

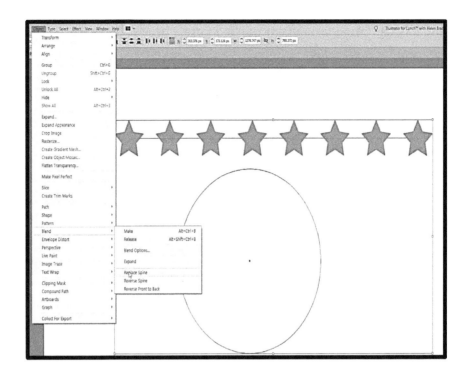

Let's just have a quick look at what these spines are about. When we click on this blend there's a line through it, and that is the spine. What we're saying to Illustrator is we know you've got a spine here but we'd like to replace this with the one we've got here so that's what this replaced spine is all about.

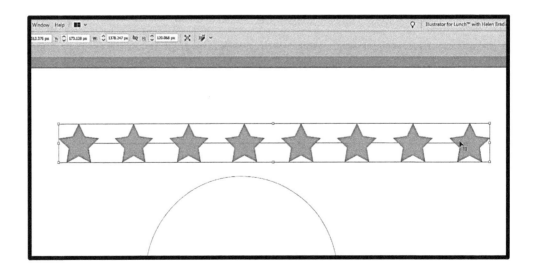

Back to our illustration, we'll select both shapes, go to Object > Blend > Replace spine, and what happens is that the stars are then placed around the circle.

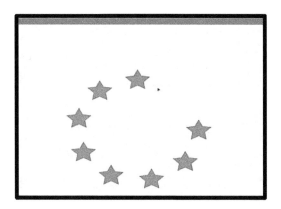

After selecting our blend with its new spine we can go back to the Blend Tool, turn preview on and we can increase or decrease the stars. Increasing and decreasing the stars is just making more stars but it's not filling in the gap. If we want to fill a gap in a closed shape, whether it be a circle, square, triangle, or whatever you're putting your blend around, you have to do what is called "Cutting this shape." You have to cut it and then it's going to work perfectly so we'll go over to the Scissors Tool and then we'll find the anchor point here. On a circle, there'll be an anchor point at the top, bottom, and either side. We are going to locate the one at the top and we're just going to click to cut it.

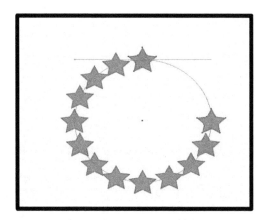

As soon as we cut it, the stars or the blend is now going all the way around the shape and of course, this is still a blend.

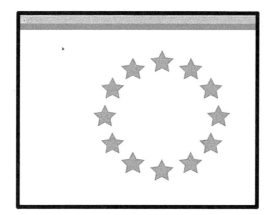

If we go to the Layers palette we're going to see that it is still a blend - we've got two stars and our spine this time instead of being aligned as fine as a circle but this is a blend. These are not individual shapes so they're also editable still.

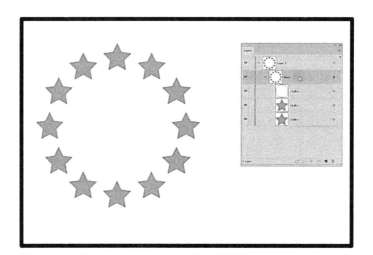

If we change the color of the other star to blue, we'll get a transition from the original pink star all the way around to a blue star. We can also double-click on the Blending options then go back to Specified steps and we can add more or fewer steps. While doing this, we can see that this is a live effect - these stars are changing color as they're being added to the design.

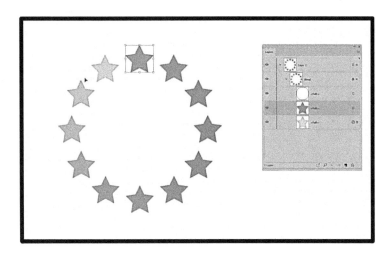

Once you're ready to settle on your design, once you're ready to bake this in and get individual stars then of course you're going to do exactly as we did before. You're going to select your blend and then expand that blend so now you have individual stars grouped in the Layers panel but each one of these is an individual star that you can then do other things with.

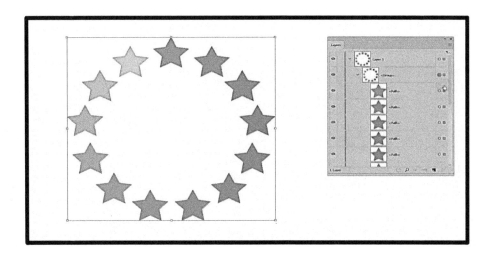

With that, you now know how to use the Blend Tool, make edits to the blend that you have created, replace a spine, and importantly break the objects out of a blend if you want to be able to deal with them independently.

Review Questions

1. How can you make your design look like it has light or dark areas using Adobe Illustrator?

2. Explain the process of creating patterns in Adobe Illustrator, and when this is useful.

3. What are the steps to make things look like they're smoothly blending in Adobe Illustrator and how can this make your design look better?

CHAPTER 12

INSTALLING AND APPLYING BRUSHES

Brushes are a really important part of Illustrator that can help you create complex designs more simply and can speed up your design creation process. In this chapter, we are going to show you the very basics of how to install, use, and save brushes in Adobe Illustrator.

The Brushes panel

Let's begin with the Brushes panel, which is where you can find Brushes in Illustrator. To open this panel, navigate to Window > Brushes or use the F5 keyboard shortcut.

In this panel, you will find all five types of brushes that can be used in Illustrator. Calligraphy brushes and Scatter brushes are displayed in a square thumbnail box while Art brushes, Bristle brushes, and Pattern brushes are displayed in a horizontal rectangle.

Let's have a look at what each of these buttons in the Brush panel does. Using the leftmost button, you can access different Brush libraries on your computer or save brushes from your Brushes panel. More information regarding the settings will be provided at the end of the chapter when you have learned how to design your brushes. Let's move on to the next button, which allows you to conveniently open the Libraries panel. These four buttons can be used to delete a brush from the brushes panel, create a new brush, change the settings of an existing brush on a route, or simply remove a brush from a path. All of these commands are also available in the drop-down menu alongside those selections. This menu allows you to alter the display of your brushes in the Brushes panel, modify which brushes are shown in the Brushes panel, and pick unused brushes to conveniently clear the Brushes panel.

Using a brush

Now that you know where to find brushes let's see how you can use one. Select the PaintBrush Tool from your toolbar or use the keyboard shortcut B, select a brush from the Brushes panel then simply click and drag to create your PaintBrush stroke.

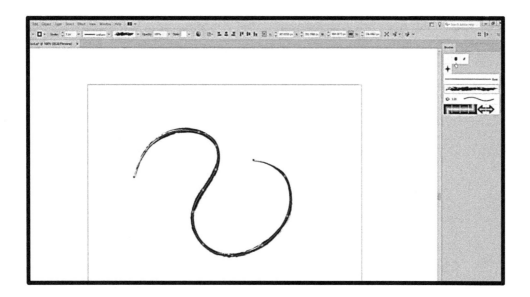

To apply a brush to an existing pad, first choose the pad and then click the brush you want to apply from the Brushes panel. Remove this pad, if you have one, then double-click the PaintBrush Tool to enter the window where you may view the options for this tool.

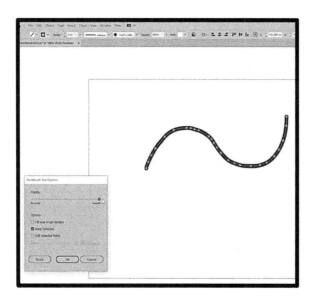

When you drag the Fidelity slider to the left, the path you're creating becomes more true to your input. If you drag the slider to the right, Illustrator smoothes your sketched path.

If you check the "Fill new brush strokes" option, the path you make will also have a fill color. If you change the fill color to red, you'll see that after you draw the path and finish it, you'll get this red fill. If you want the path to remain selected after you've finished drawing it, simply tick the "keep selected" option.

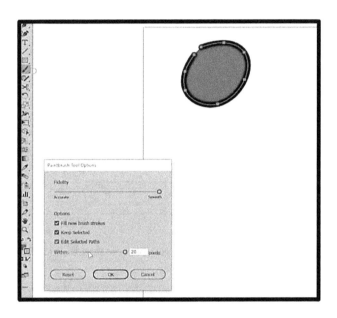

The third option allows you to edit a path on top of a previously constructed path within the pixel range you choose using this slider. If you want to draw a line and are dissatisfied with your first try, all you have to do is draw a second one on top of the original one, and when you release the button, the second attempt will replace the first. In addition to the settings from the PaintBrush Tool options window, you can hit the SHIFT key before you start drawing a path to easily generate straight and oblique pads, or you can press the ALT/OPTION key after you start drawing a path to ensure that your path is closed once you release the button of the mouse.

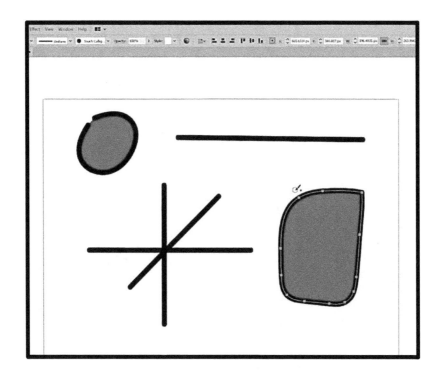

The different types of brushes

Now that you know where to find brushes and how to use them, let's learn more about the different types of brushes and how you can create your brushes.

The Calligraphic brush

Let's start with the calligraphic brush. To create a new brush, simply click the "New brush" **button**. Make sure the Calligraphic Brush box is checked, and then click **OK** to access the window where you may customize your new brush. Type a name for this new brush, then click **OK**. Your new brush will appear in the Brushes panel.

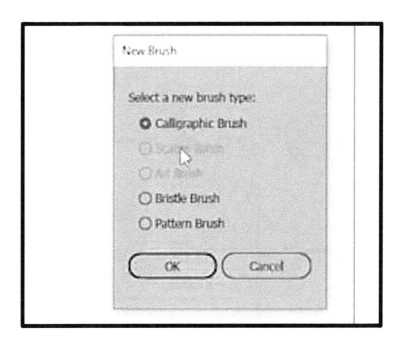

Select the PaintBrush Tool and your Calligraphic brush from the Brushes panel to draw a simple path. The color of a Calligraphic brush depends on the stroke color that you choose to select. You can change it to another color and then double-click your brush to edit it.

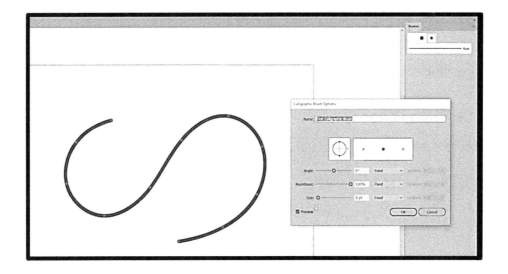

Make sure the "Preview box" is ticked to see the changes as you alter the settings of your brush. Lowering the roundness value creates a flatter brush, while the angle and size sliders allow you to change the angle of rotation and diameter of your brush. Once you're finished, click OK to apply all of your changes. Double-click your Calligraphic brush to boost its roundness to 100%, and now let's look at how the variables in these drop-down boxes function. Most of these capabilities are especially beneficial while utilizing a graphics tablet. Let's focus on the size settings to first exemplify this random variable. When the size is set to 10 and the variation is 5 the size range of the brush will go between 5 and 15. So when you are drawing paths using this brush you will get random sizes varying between 5 and 15. The other 5 variables can only be used if you own a graphics tablet.

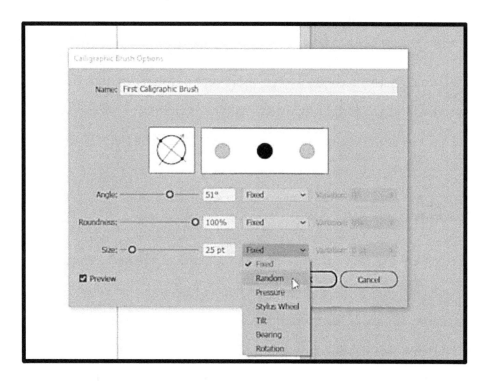

Let us start with pressure and see how it works. With the same size values, the brush's size range will be 5 to 15, depending on the pressure applied with the drawing stylus. When you press harder, the brush thickens, and when you release the pressure, the brush thins. Let's return to the Calligraphic brush and focus on the next variables.

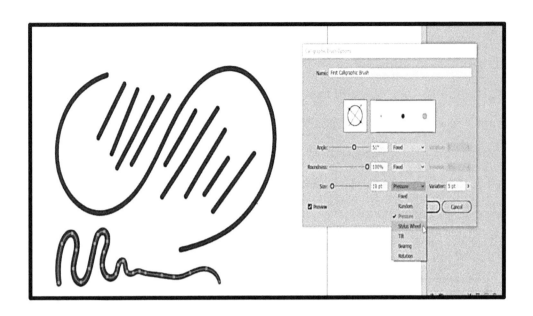

The Stylus wheel variable is created to be used with a brush pen that has a stylus wheel. The brush size will vary based on the manipulation of the stylus wheel. With these other three variables, the brush size will vary based on the tilt, the bearing, or the rotation of the pen's tip.

The Scatter brush

Scatter brushes are the second type of brush that can be created in Illustrator. To make one, you'll need a shape or combination of forms. Remember that when creating a Scatter brush, you cannot apply gradients or effects. In this example, we will use a star. Select your star, click the "New brush" button, select the Scatter Brush box, and then click OK to open the panel where you may customize your new brush. Enter a name, click OK, and your new Scatter brush will appear in the Brushes panel.

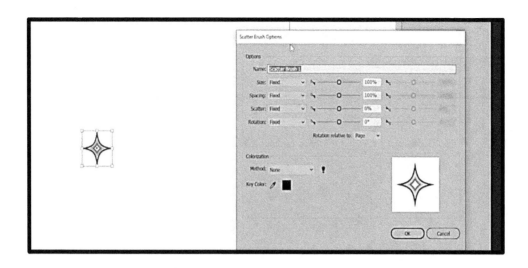

To draw a simple route, use the PaintBrush Tool from your toolbar, and then double-click your Scatter brush to better grasp all of the settings. Make sure to enable Preview so that you can see all of the changes as you make them. These sliders allow you to adjust the size, spacing, scatter, and rotation of the Brush elements. These values are always relative to the original form that you select for your Scatter brush. When you select a random size, you may use these two sliders to establish a range of sizes for the Brush elements. To use one of these versions, you'll need a graphics tablet, much like the other brushes. The "Rotation relative to" drop-down menu allows you to select the angle of rotation for Brush components relative to the page or the route.

Let's keep it relative to the page. A Scatter brush's color is determined by the stroke color and colorization method selected from this menu. The same restrictions apply to Art and Pattern Brushes. Let's look at the colorization approach and open this drop-down menu. When you choose Tints, black is replaced by the stroke color. Colors that are not black are substituted by tints of the stroke color, but white remains unchanged. Selecting Tints and Shades will replace the existing colors with tints and shades of the stroke color. Black and white does not change. Selecting Hue shift will replace the existing colors with the stroke color based on this key color.

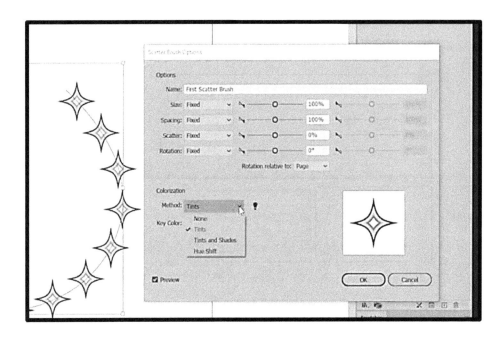

By default, the most present color from your brush is said to be the key color. To change this key color just click the Eyedropper icon and click the color that you want to be set as the key from the preview. The sections from the brush that use the key color will be replaced with the stroke color, and the other colors will be replaced with variations of the stroke color; again, black and white do not change. Another way to understand better how these colorization methods work is to always click these Tips button

Art brush

The third sort of brush that may be created in Illustrator is the Art brush. Remember that while saving an Art brush, you cannot utilize gradients or effects. Click the "**New brush"
button**, select the **Art brush box**, and then click **OK** to open the window where you may

configure your new brush. Change the name and click **OK**; your new Art brush will appear in the Brushes section.

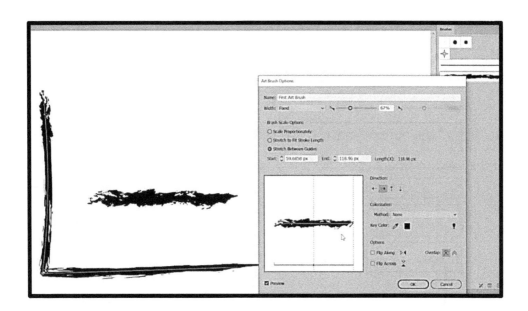

To draw a simple path, use the PaintBrush Tool and your Art brush, and then double-click your Art brush to better grasp all of the parameters. The slider allows you to raise or decrease the width of your brush relative to the original shape, and the Pen tablet variables, such as Calligraphic brushes, and Scatter brushes, can be selected from a drop-down menu.

You can resize the brush to match the proportions of the original shape or stretch it to accommodate the length of the path. The third option allows you to specify a region of the brush that should stretch. If you move the guide to the center, the section on the right will stretch while the one on the left will remain in its original shape. Check "Stretch to Fit," set the width to 100%, and then focus on the Direction option.

Using these arrow buttons, you can change the brush's orientation relative to the path. The blue arrow helps you comprehend how the brush is applied to the path. When it comes to colorization, Art brushes use the same settings as Scatter brushes. With these bottom options, you can easily flip your brush along the pad, across the pad or you can fix this unwanted overlap using the second Overlap button.

The Bristle brush

Bristle brushes are the fourth type of brush that may be created in Illustrator. To make one, simply click the **"New brush" button**, select the **Bristle brush option**, and then click **OK** to enter the window where you can configure your new brush. As with the other brushes, you can alter the name, then click **OK**, and your new Bristle brush will appear in the Brushes panel.

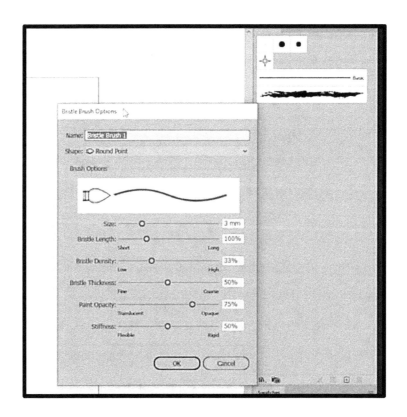

Select the PaintBrush Tool to design a simple pad with your Bristle brush, and then double-click it to view all of the settings. You may select the style of the brush tip from the Shapes drop-down box; these options are rather simple and provide an infinite number of possibilities for creating whatever Bristle brush you require. You can choose the brush size, bristle length, bristle density (calculated based on the numbers you enter for the first two options), bristle thickness, paint opacity, and bristle rigidity. When you are done, click OK. Before we move on you should know that the color of a bristle brush depends on the straw color that you choose to select.

The Pattern brush

The final type of brush that may be created in Illustrator is the Pattern brush. When storing a pattern brush, you cannot utilize gradients or effects like you can with regular brushes. Select the desired forms, click the "New brush" button, select the Pattern brush box, and then click OK to open the panel where you may customize your new Pattern brush. Type a name and click OK, and your new Pattern brush will appear in the Brushes section.

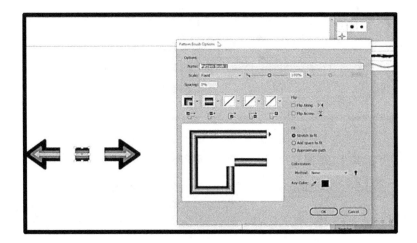

Select the PaintBrush Tool to create a simple path with your Pattern brush, and then double-click it to see all of the possibilities available here. Make sure the Preview box is checked, and then focus on the scale options. Using this slider, you can change the breadth of the brush in relation to the original shape you choose for your pattern brush. Return it to 100 percent, and, as with the other brushes, use the Scale drop-down option to access the tablet variables.

You can add space between the tiles that make up your Pattern brush, flip your Pattern brush along the pad or across the pad, and use these Fit choices to control how the tiles behave. The "Stretch to Fit" option will stretch the tiles to fit the entire length of the pad. "Add space to fit" will increase the spacing between the tiles while keeping the tile size the same. "Approximate path" will approximate the nearest path required to perfectly fit the tiles while preserving their size.

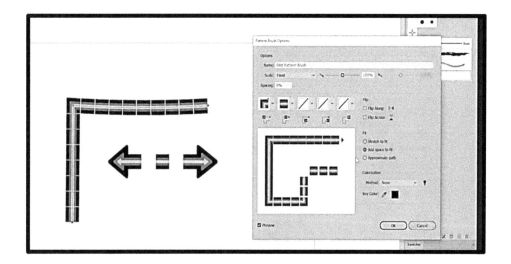

Pattern brushes use the same colorization parameters as Art brushes and scatter brushes. By employing these tile buttons, you can customize the appearance of certain portions of a Pattern brush. This side tile is created using the major parts that you need to store your Pattern brush, and Illustrator generates tiles for the corners of a Pattern brush. You can choose them from the dropdown menu. You must design the start and end tiles yourself.

How to create and apply tiles to a Pattern brush

Let's show you how you can create your tiles and how you can apply them to a Pattern brush. Select the elements you want to use and simply drag them inside the Swatches panel to save them as patterns. Get back to the Brushes panel and double-click your Pattern brush. From the start tile select "New pattern Swatch 1," and from the end tile select "New pattern Swatch 2." Click ok to apply the changes.

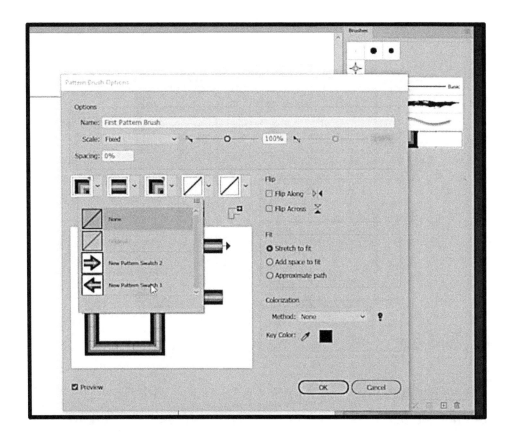

Select the PaintBrush Tool and draw some smooth arrows. Keep in mind that you can always alter the colorization to Tints to vary the color of your arrow. In some circumstances, the corner tiles that Illustrator generates for your Pattern brush may not appear as you expect, and you will need to build your corner tiles. Throughout this chapter, we mentioned that gradients cannot be used for brushes; but, you can use blends; you can make a blend that appears like a gradient and use it to create a brush.

Loading your Brushes

When you want to load a set of brushes, simply double-click the Illustrator document and focus on the Brushes panel where you will notice that your brushes are already loaded and ready to use. If you can't see this panel all you have to do is go to Window in the menu bar and select Brushes.

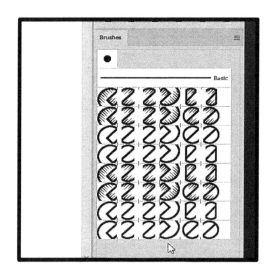

Applying your brush

Now that you have your brushes, let's see how easy it is to apply them. Select the **Ellipse Tool from the toolbar,** draw a simple route, and then select a brush from the Brushes panel to apply to your path. Much more typically, you can utilize the PaintBrush Tool to see how your brush handles different angles and curved pathways.

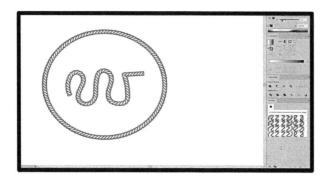

Saving your brush

Now let's say that you'll only need the top four brushes, remove the button for brushes, and to use these brushes in another document you'll have to save them. To do this, all you have to do is click the first button in the bottom right corner and go to 'Save brushes" or you can open the flier menu from the Brushes panel and go to "Save brush library."

You can save your brushes in the Preset folder or you can select a different one (for this illustration we'll save them in the Preset folder), type in a name for your new set of brushes, and click Save.

Accessing your saved brushes

If you saved your brushes in the Preset folder, and you click the first button in the lower right corner and select User Defined, you will see your brushes. Alternatively, from the Brushes panel, open the flyout menu and select Open Brush Library and User Defined, where you will locate your set of brushes. Simply click on it to bring up the panel containing your brushes.

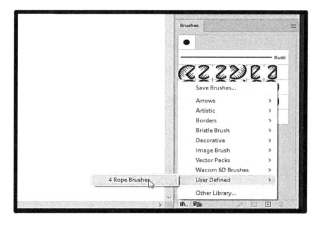

When you choose to save your brushes in a different folder you can access them by going to "Other Library." You have the same command in the menu of the Brushes panel.

The way you organize your brushes is entirely up to you. Aside from your stored brushes, you'll see some Preset collections of brushes included with Illustrator. You can load any of these brush libraries with a single click. Keep in mind that you may use these arrow buttons to conveniently move between the Preset brush libraries, and after you've found the brush you need, simply click it to apply it to the specified route.

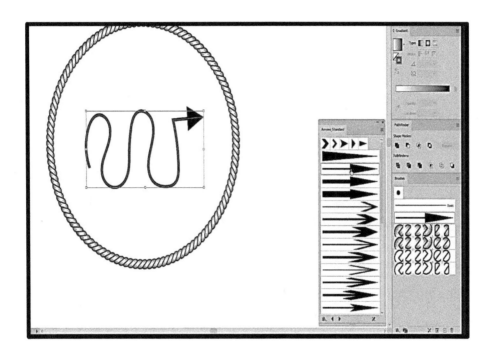

Changing the color of a brush

To alter the color of the brush, simply change the stroke color. You can do it from the Color panel or by double-clicking the Stroke color wheel in the toolbar, selecting a color, and clicking OK. To modify the color of a more intricate brush, utilize the "Recolor artwork" option. Choose your path, then click the **Recolor Artwork button** in the Control panel or navigate to **Edit > Edit Colors > Recolor artwork.**

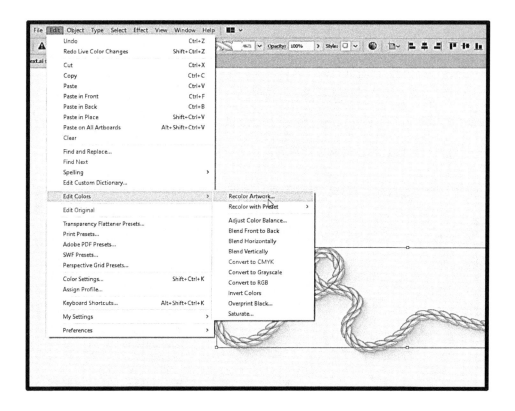

Click the Advanced Options button to get access to all the settings of the "Recolor artwork" option, and using these color buttons here you can change each color one by one or you can switch to the Edit mode and use these color handles to change all the colors of the brush at once.

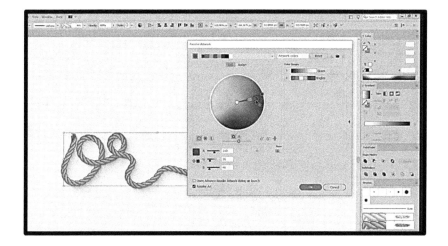

Changing the size of your brush

To change the size of a brush all you have to do is adjust the Stroke weight from the Control panel.

Applying gradients on brushes

You should realize that gradients cannot be applied to Illustrator brushes. If you need to accomplish this, you will need to widen your brush. Before expanding the brush, remove the fill color (if applicable) and then select Object > Expand Appearance. Using the first button in the Pathfinder panel, combine the resulting collection of forms and fill your shape with a radial gradient.

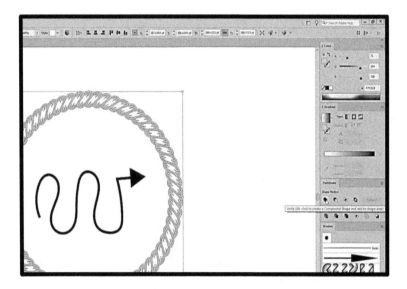

You can adjust the gradient slider by 80%, change the color mode to RGB, and select your color. Then, choose the other gradient slider, change the hue mode to RGB, and choose a darker hue.

Editing a certain instance of the brush

Before we wrap up this chapter, remember that you can use the Stroke Options option to adjust a specific instance of the brush while leaving the other strokes unchanged. Make the desired changes, then click OK to observe that only the selected path is edited.

Review Questions

1. How do you install brushes in Adobe Illustrator, and why is this helpful for making your artwork better?

2. Explain how to use brushes on your artwork in Adobe Illustrator, and give examples of how different brushes can change the way they look.

3. Are there any important things to remember when using brushes in Adobe Illustrator?

CHAPTER 13

APPLYING EFFECTS

In this chapter, we are going to be explaining every effect of Adobe Illustrator. Before we proceed, some things you have to know are:

- Effects follow a non-destructive workflow, which means any changes they make are reversible - you can always edit, hide, or delete them.
- Effects interact with each other, so you can stack multiple effects on a single object for increasingly complex visuals.
- Effects and the Appearance Panel work together. You can use the panel to view, edit, hide, delete, and move effects on any object.

Exploring the various effects

3D and Materials effect

The 3D and Materials effect has so many customization options that it has its panel.

There are 3 different tabs on the 3D effect: Object, Materials, and Lighting.

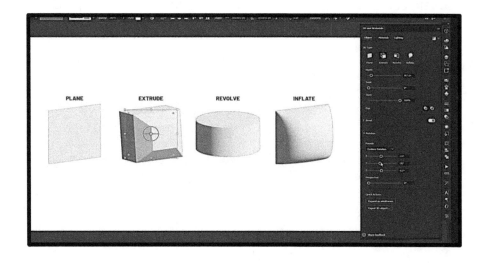

- **The Object tab has the most important setting:** the 3D Type. This is where you may define and customize the shape of your 3D item, and each 3D type has a unique set of customization choices. Below the 3D Type section, you can add and alter bevels, and at the bottom, you may rotate the object and change the camera angle.

- The Materials tab allows you to apply different materials and textures to the item. You have the default material, which is quite simple and lacks texturing, as well as a selection of Adobe Substance's more intricate and realistic materials. At the bottom, you can alter the materials' attributes and appearance.

- Finally, the Lighting tab allows you to add and configure light sources. You can adjust the light settings with the sliders or choose one of the presets. There is a list of all the light sources in the scene, and you can add new ones by selecting the "Add Light" option. At the very bottom, you can enable shadows, which make the item much more lifelike. You can enable rendering or fine-tune it under the render options, which are located in the top right corner of the panel.

3D Classic

The classic 3D effect is a legacy effect that has been replaced by the new 3D and Materials effect. It still allows you to model 3D vectors, but it lacks the new panel's ray tracing capabilities. Unless your computer has problems with performance, we recommend utilizing the new 3D effect instead of this one.

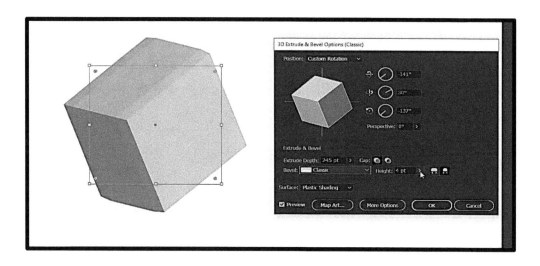

Convert-to-Shape effect

The "Convert to Shape" effect converts the selected item to one of three shapes: rectangle, rounded rectangle, or ellipse. The form size can be absolute, which means that the final shape will be the same size as the original item, or relative, which means that the final shape will add width and height.

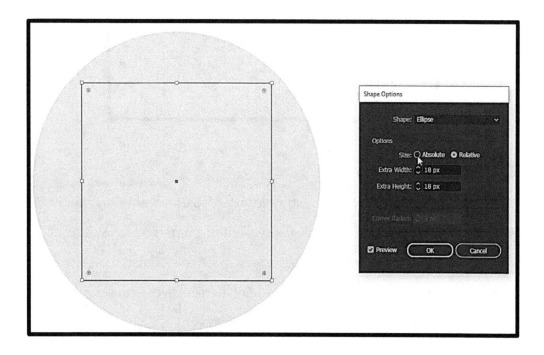

This effect is not particularly useful on its own. However, when combined with other effects or text, it can produce interesting results. For example, you can add a new fill to a text object and use the "Convert to Shape" effect to create a box behind the text that automatically scales as you type.

Crop Marks effect

The Crop Marks effect adds four crop marks on the corners of the selected object. Crop marks indicate where you want the printed paper to be cut.

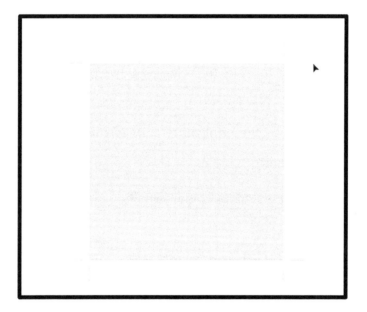

Free Distort effect

The Free distort effect lets you skew and deform an object in any way you like. In the Effects window, drag the four control points in the corners to alter the object. It's comparable to the Free Transform Tool, but a little more challenging to use. Nonetheless, it's a valuable non-destructive alternative for adding perspective - and yes, the word "non-destructive" will appear frequently throughout this chapter.

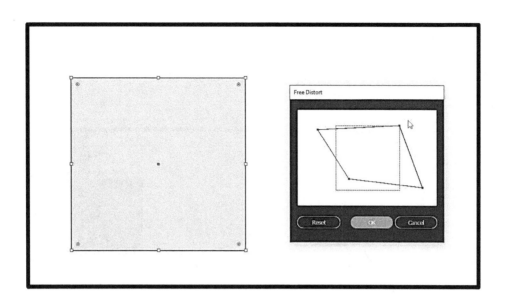

This is also an excellent occasion to discuss the stacking order of effects in the Appearance Panel. The Appearance Panel displays and organizes all of an object's elements, such as fills, strokes, opacity, and effects, into layers. Changing the sequence of these layers can affect the final appearance of the item. Let's take a square for example. It presently contains two layers: a fill and a stroke. If we use the Free Distort effect, it will appear at the bottom of the stack and distort the object.

We can also add a Drop Shadow effect which we'll talk about later in this chapter. It appears once again at the bottom of the stack and adds a shadow that matches the shape of the object after the distortion.

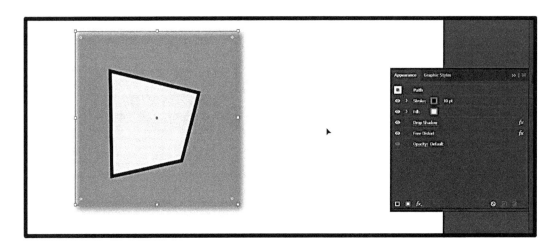

But what happens if we move the shadow above the distortion? The result is strange, but it makes sense when we think about it: we first apply the shadow to the object, which is a square, and then deform it. Another amazing feature: we may add effects to individual fills or strokes. For example, if we drag the Free Distort effect into the Fill layer, only the Fill will be warped; the stroke will remain square. Similarly, moving it inside the stroke layer will simply deform the stroke. The same is true for the Drop Shadow effect, which only affects the stroke when we move it inside the stroke layer. So many different looks with just two effects, right?

Pucker & Bloat effect

The Pucker & Bloat effect causes the anchor points to migrate toward or away from the object's center. Dragging the slider to the left expands the anchor points, making the object pointed. Dragging it to the right causes the anchor points to go inward, rounding the item.

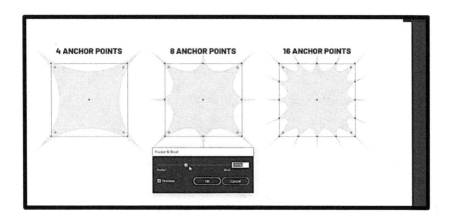

Pucker is excellent for creating sparkles and stars, whilst Bloat is ideal for creating adorable flowers. Because this effect manipulates anchor points, even if two items appear to be identical, the number of anchor points they have affects how the effect appears.

The Roughen effect

The Roughen effect adds a random texture to strokes and fills, creating a hand-drawn look. This is a cool effect for when you need something to look more natural and hand-made, or just to add visual interest.

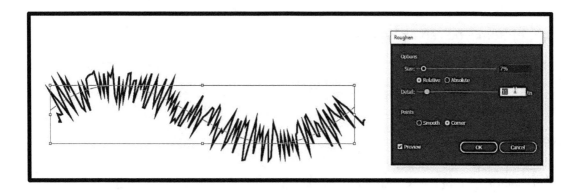

There are two main controls on the effect: Size and detail are most easily understood by gazing at a single line. Size creates distortion away from the original path, whereas detail distorts the path. A straight line can be thought of as both vertical and horizontal distortion. You have the choice of using relative or absolute size. Relative employs a percentage, whereas Absolute uses a set value. This influences how the effect scales; as the object's size increases or decreases, so does the effect. The effect remains constant even when the size is absolute.

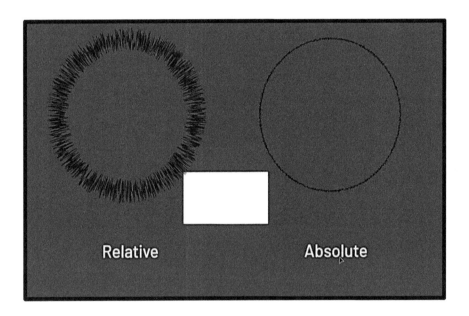

At the bottom, you can also choose if you want the distortion to have smooth curves or sharp corners. Different from the Pucker & Bloat effect, Roughen is not anchor point dependent, so even a straight line with only two anchor points will be distorted.

Transform effect

The Transform effect lets you perform simple transformations on the object, such as scaling, rotation, and position. You can modify the vertical and horizontal properties of scale and position separately. In the Options section, you can apply the effect to the object,

197

the pattern, or both, as well as reflect and transform at random. This is one of those effects that appears basic on the surface but gives you a vast range of options for creating highly intricate things.

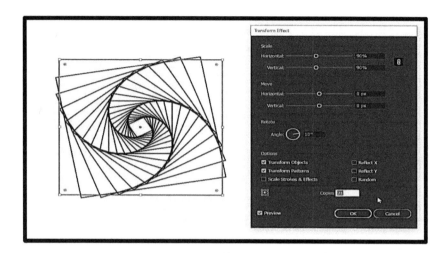

At the very bottom of the Effects window, you can generate copies, and the amazing thing is that each copy stacks another instance of the effect. So, if you rotate 10 degrees and scale down 10%, each successive copy you add will be rotated another 10 degrees and scaled down 10% more, allowing you to build stunning geometric patterns with a few clicks. Just be careful when making copies, because this effect can have a significant influence on performance depending on the complexity of the item and the number of copies you make.

Tweak effect

The Tweak effect moves anchor points and handles randomly, for a more chaotic look. It's a very odd effect and even though it is random, you do have sliders to control how much distortion you want, either vertically or horizontally, and if you want to use relative or absolute values.

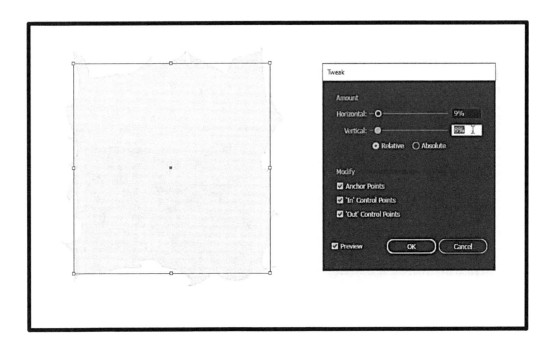

Essentially, when you apply the effect, it creates a random ratio between each anchor point and handle, thus even if you raise the distortion, the ratio remains constant. It's worth mentioning that each time you use the effect, a new random seed is generated, so even if you have numerous objects with the same anchor points, they will all appear different.

This effect functions similarly to the Roughen effect, but it is anchor point dependent, so, like Pucker & Bloat, the number of anchor points and their placement will determine how the Tweak effect appears.

At the bottom of the Effects box, you'll discover choices to change anchor points or handles, both within and outside. However, the illustrator refers to them as "control points" for some reason. Leaving anchor points unchecked leaves all anchor points in place while only moving the handles, and vice versa. To summarize, it is useful for creating random scribbles or wild-looking forms.

Twist effect

The best way to explain the Twist effect is to imagine that you are placing the object inside a vortex. That's all it does. This effect only has one control, which is the angle, and the more you turn it up, the more twisted the object becomes.

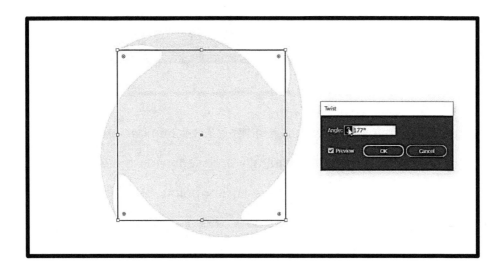

You may see some uses for it, but if you set the angle to a high value, objects start looking the same. It also creates some imperfections along the curves so keep that in mind.

 ZigZag effect

The ZigZag effect is similar to the Roughen Effect, except that it distorts in a zig-zag pattern rather than randomly. Other than that, all controls are the same. Size distorts vertically away from the path, whereas segments distort horizontally along it. Relative and Absolute toggle between percentages and fixed numbers, and at the bottom, you can leave the zig-zag sharp or rounded.

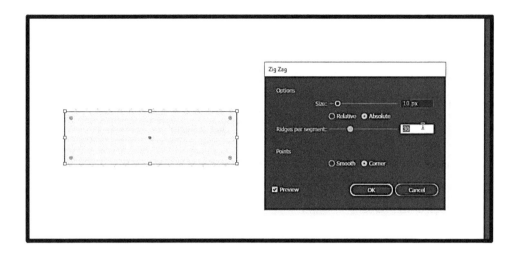

The disadvantage of this effect is that it adds a fixed number of ridges to each path segment, thus unless your object has identically sized segments, this effect is uninteresting. The solution to this problem is to add more anchor points, but this is not how it should function. Zig-zag is a great effect. Despite its restrictions, it is ideal for creating fantastic badges and stamps, as well as adding detail to a simple shape.

Offset Path effect

The Offset Path effect is very self-explanatory. When applied, it shifts the path by a given amount, either inwards or outwards. The Effects window contains three settings. First, you can specify how far the path will be offset, and it's worth noting that you can even enter negative values to offset inward. Then you can select the corner type. There are three options: miter, round, and bevel. Finally, you can set a limit for the miter join, which is the angle at which a sharp corner becomes a miter.

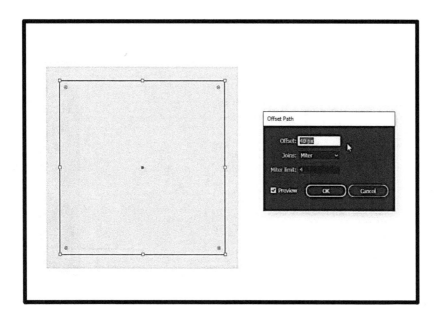

The Offset Path effect is very handy in workflows where you're layering numerous fills, strokes, and effects, and you need one layer to be larger than the others to see it. You could also use the Transform effect to raise the size of a layer, which may work for some forms, but Transform would just scale the object up, whereas Offset Path will grow the path uniformly throughout the object.

Outline Object effect

The Outline Object effect is mostly used for adding strokes to photographs. If you've ever attempted to add an outline to an image in Illustrator, you know it's impossible. However, when you select the stroke in the Appearance panel and apply the Outline Object effect, the stroke appears.

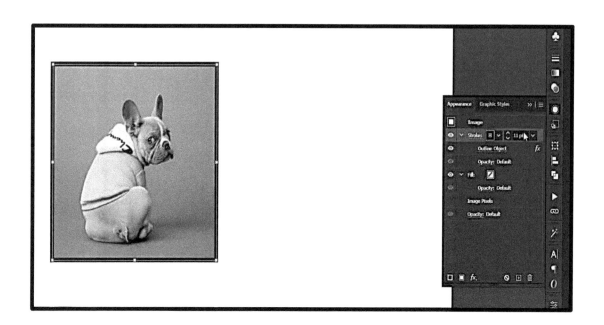

You can also use this effect to show a more precise bounding box around text objects. However, you also need to open the Preferences Menu and toggle "Use Preview Bounds." This makes such a huge difference.

Outline Stroke effect

The Outline Stroke effect, on the other hand, is far more practical and simple to grasp. This effect changes the stroke into a filled object, similar to the Expand option in the Object Menu. This can dramatically alter how effects are applied to the object. Effects like Roughen generate very different results depending on whether Outline Stroke is used or not. Without an Outline Stroke, the Roughen effect affects the original path that the stroke follows. When the Outline Stroke is applied, the stroke transforms into a rectangle, and the Roughen effect alters the outer edges of the stroke rather than the original route.

Pathfinder effect

The Pathfinder effect allows you to combine forms in a non-destructive way by using the Pathfinder panel's Boolean functions. To use this effect, group at least two things. Once you've picked the group, navigate to the Effects menu and select the desired operation. If you don't get it right the first time, you can expand your options by accessing the Effects window from the Appearance panel. At the top of the window, you'll see a drop-down menu with all accessible operations.

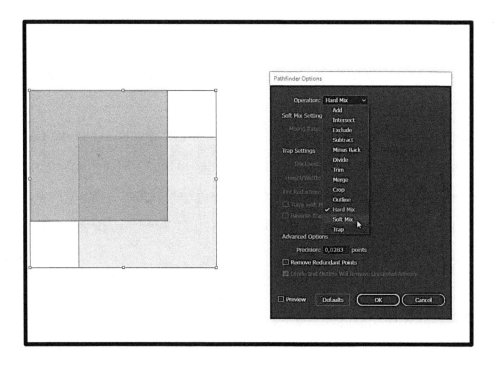

The majority of them mix shapes in some way, with the last three dealing with color, which we shall cover momentarily. Pathfinder operations are too numerous and complex to explain, therefore we propose that you simply scroll through them until you get the desired outcome. Some are simple to comprehend, such as Intersect, which deletes everything except the sections that overlap, and Exclude, which does the opposite.

As for the last three options:

- First, you have "Hard Mix." This operation examines two objects' color channels (RGB or CMYK) and selects the darkest value from each channel to produce a new color. If we use blue and yellow as examples, the darkest numbers are 56 for red, 189 for green, and 88 for blue. When we compare the resulting green to the green from the Hard Mix procedure, we can see that they are the same.

- Despite the similarity in name, Soft Mix is not exactly the opposite of Hard Mix. Soft Mix reveals the underlying colors through the overlapping artwork. In practice, it makes the yellow object translucent, but only where the two items intersect. If you enlarge the objects using the Object menu, you'll notice that both Hard Mix and Soft Mix separate them into component faces.

- Finally, we have Trap, which is a little more complicated and may not be as widely used. When two overlapping colors are printed in the CMYK color system, they may leave a white space between them. Trapping generates a slight overlap between the hues to avoid this from occurring.

Rasterize effect

The Rasterize effect is a non-destructive way to Rasterize objects. Rasterize means to turn into a raster image, an image made out of pixels, like a JPEG or a PNG. The other option is to select Rasterize on the Object menu, but this way you won't be able to toggle the rasterization on and off or continue to edit the vector object. It'll become an image.

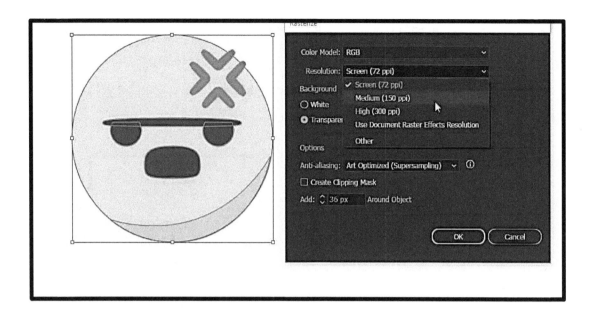

The Rasterize effect allows you to examine the rasterized object while still editing it and applying other effects. You can select the color model and resolution in the Effects box, located at the top. Typically, you'll need 72 for digital and 150 or 300 for printing. In the background section, you can leave it translucent or fill it with white. In the Options area, you can enable anti-aliasing, either for graphics or text. Anti-aliasing is a technique for smoothing rough edges and reducing pixelation that involves mixing colors along object edges. Finally, you can offset the outer bounds of the image by how many pixels you input here, and check the "Create Clipping Mask" box to automatically create a clipping mask using the shape of the vector itself.

Drop Shadow effect

Drop Shadow is possibly the most commonly used effect in Illustrator. It's a simple and easy-to-understand effect, but there are a few interesting aspects to it. Drop Shadow is self-explanatory: it casts a shadow behind an object. You can control the opacity of the shadow, the X and Y positions, and the blur, which determines how soft the shadow is. At the bottom, you can select a specific color and a darkness level. The darkness option uses the color of the object itself and gradually adds black to it, creating a shadow that has a little bit of the object's color in it - in our case, a shadow that is a little bit yellow, and not straight up black. This looks way more realistic.

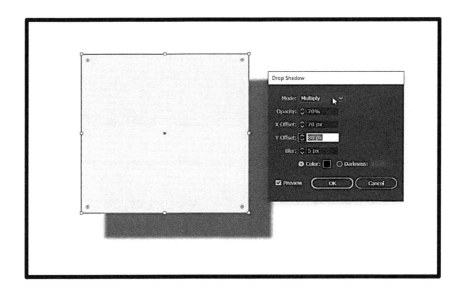

You can also change the blending mode of the effect. Blending modes are ways to blend a color with everything that's below it. By default, the effect comes with the multiply effect selected, which darkens what's below but if you select the Screen blending mode and choose a brighter color, you can turn the drop shadow into a glow effect. The Drop Shadow effect is also the first raster effect on the list, which means that the effect itself is a raster image and not a vector. You can see that by zooming into the shadow to see the pixels showing up. This happens with every effect that requires some sort of blur. The resolution of raster effects is selected when you create a new document. However, if you want to change the resolution later, you can do it by going to the Effects menu and choosing Document > Raster Effects Settings.

Feather effect

If you're familiar with Photoshop, you already know what Feather does. If not, don't worry it is super simple: the Feather effect blurs the edges of the object in a soft fade to transparent.

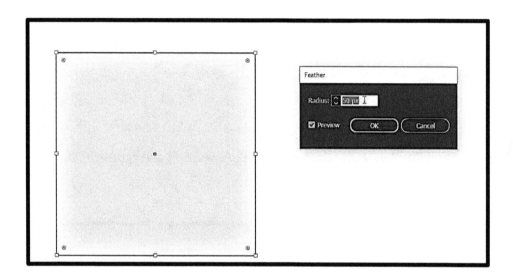

Inner Glow effect

The Inner Glow effect is like Drop Shadow but inside the object. There's not much to control in this effect - you can choose blending mode, color, opacity, and blur, and you already know how all of this works from the Drop Shadow effect. At the bottom, you have the Options Center and Edge, and toggling between them inverts the starting point of the glow. If you set the blending mode to multiply and pick a dark color, you can also use this effect as an inner shadow.

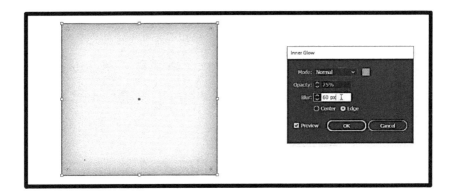

Outer Glow effect

If Inner Glow was like Drop Shadow, Outer Glow is Drop Shadow, just without the X and Y position. It's Drop Shadow with position set to 0. Absolutely the same effect, no difference at all.

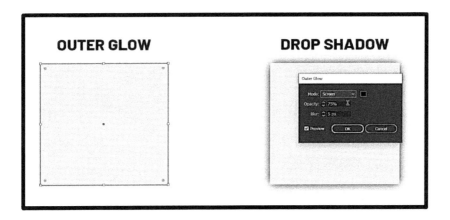

Round Corners effect

The Round Corners effect lost a bit of its use with the introduction of live corners, but it's still a great way to round corners in a non-destructive way. The effect is as simple as it gets: it rounds sharp corners. You have one option in the Effects window, which is the radius of the roundness.

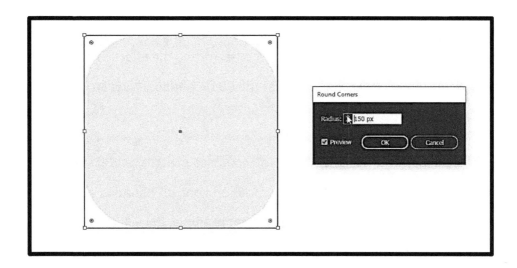

Scribble effect

Scribble is such a fun little effect. It's the easiest way to turn your design into a sketch or even a child drawing. The effect turns any fill or stroke into scribbles, and there are a lot of customization options.

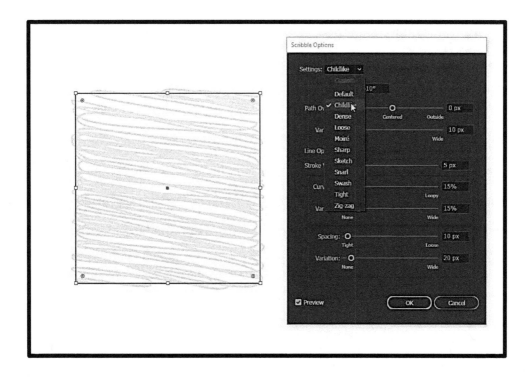

First, we have a drop-down menu with a ton of presets. Some are more contained, some are more chaotic. They're a great place to start customizing the effect. Then, we can choose the angle at which the scribbles go, as well as the Path Overlap. This is an Offset Path inside the Scribble effect.

If you drag the slider to the left, it offsets the scribbles inwards, and if you drag it to the right, it offsets outwards. Below, there is a Variation control that adds some randomness to Path Overlap. If you set Variation to 5 pixels, for example, the value you selected in Path Overlap will randomly fluctuate between -5 and +5 for every line of the scribble, giving it a more loose, natural, and hand-drawn look.

Then, we have some line options. You can change the stroke width, curviness, and spacing. Stroke width is self-explanatory, and while it, unfortunately, doesn't have a variation control, curviness and spacing do. Curviness controls the behavior of the scribble at the end of each stroke. If set to angular, the end of the stroke will be a sharp corner, and dragging the slider to the right adds curviness, making it, again, more loose and natural. Variation will work the same way as previously explained, adding randomness.

You can keep curviness at 0 and then add a little bit of variation. Spacing controls the space in between each stroke of the scribble, from tight to loose. This severely affects performance, since a tighter scribble will have more lines drawn. Be careful not to drag this slider to the left, as it will draw so many lines that Illustrator might crash. It's worth mentioning that you can apply separate Scribble effects on the fill and the stroke through the Appearance Panel, since the settings that look good on the fill, might not on the stroke.

SVG Filters

SVG Filters are effects aimed at web design. SVG effects differ from their bitmap counterparts in that they are XML-based and resolution-independent. An SVG effect is nothing more than a series of XML properties that describe various mathematical operations. The effect is rendered to the target object instead of the source graphic.

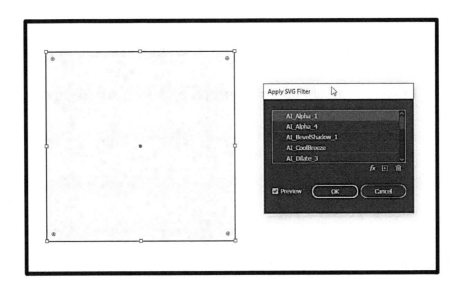

Illustrator comes with a list of default, pre-installed filters, which you can access by clicking on the effect on the Appearance Panel. On the Effects window, you can access the XML code by clicking on the FX button, or write your code and create your filters by clicking on the plus button.

Warp effect

Warp is once again a non-destructive approach to apply an Object menu item, this time an Envelope Distort with Warp. The Warp effect distorts the object in a variety of ways using a mesh that can be selected from the Effects menu or the Effects window.

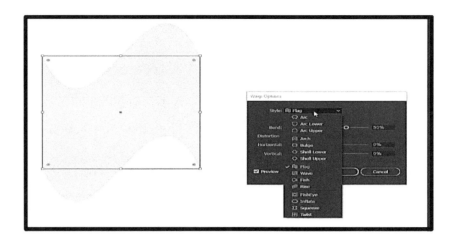

After selecting the style you want for the distortion, you can use the Bend slider to change the amount of distortion you want to apply. Using negative values will invert the mesh, distorting the object in the opposite direction. You can also apply the bend to the object either horizontally or vertically. In the distortion section, you can add perspective to the bend, either horizontally or vertically.

Review Questions

1. What are 5 cool effects that you can put on your artwork in Adobe Illustrator, and how do they make it look better?

2. Explain how to add shadows, 3D effects, and distortions to your artwork in Adobe Illustrator, and explain how to adjust them.

3. Give examples of how you can use effects to create a certain feeling or style in your artwork.

CHAPTER 14

GOING PRO WITH ILLUSTRATOR

In this chapter, we are going to show you all that you need to know about Illustrator's Appearance and Graphics Styles panels. After that, we will quickly look at the Creative Cloud library.

The Appearance Panel and Graphic Styles

The Appearance panel along with the Graphics Styles panel is one of the most important features in Illustrator and once you master these panels your workflow will increase greatly.

The Appearance panel

To open it you can either go to Window in the menu bar or select Appearance or you can use the SHIFT and F6 keyboard shortcut. By default, you will get a black stroke and a white field.

In the top left corner, you can find a thumbnail that represents the existing Appearance settings. If you can't see it you need to open the menu and select "Show thumbnail." If you wish to hide that thumbnail you need to select "Hide thumbnail" from this menu. You can simply click and drag it onto an object from your design whenever you wish to apply the existing Appearance settings to that object.

Next to the thumbnail, there's the title bar. In the beginning, this can be useful to know exactly the type of object that you have selected. It can be a path type, a group, or even a layer and it also lets you know if a graphic style is applied. Back to the slider bar you need to select it whenever you wish to be sure that an effect that you're about to add gets applied on the entire object, not just a particular fill or stroke from your design. Finally, you have the opacity bar. Click this opacity text to open the transparency flyout panel which can be used to adjust the opacity or the blending mode settings for the object that you have selected. Again, these changes will affect the entire object, not just a particular fill or stroke from your design.

Graphic Styles

One method is to save the Appearance settings as a Graphic Style and then use that graphic style to easily apply the same attributes to other objects. You can open the Graphic Styles panel by going to Window > Graphic Styles or you can use the SHIFT+F5 keyboard shortcut. To save a new graphic style all you have to do is click the "New Graphic Style" button to apply, select an object, and just click your graphic style. If you wish to apply the graphic style and also keep the current settings make sure that you're holding down the ALT/OPTION key as you click the graphic style. Now that we covered the basics let's focus on the rest of these buttons and see how you can use them. As with the Appearance panel, all of these commands can also be accessed via the flyout menu from the Graphics Styles panel. First, of all, you should know that the "New Graphic Style" button can also be used to duplicate a graphic style. You'll learn in a few moments why you might want to duplicate one.

This "Break Link" button goes hand in hand with the "Redefine Graphic Style" command which can be found in the flyout menu of the Appearance panel. Let's say that you apply the same graphics style for several objects from your design, select just one of these objects, focus on the Appearance panel and as you can see Illustrator lets you know that you have a graphics style applied but clicking this "Break Link" button will cut the ties between the current Appearance settings and your saved graphics style so just click this button and the graphic style will disappear from the Appearance panel.

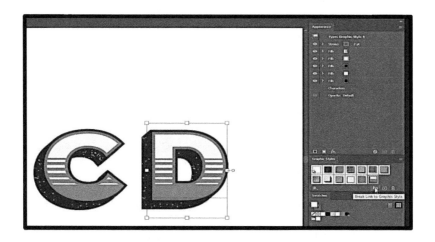

You can select another set of objects, make a quick adjustment, and now if you go to redefine graphic style your graphic style will be updated in the panel and all the instances where your graphics style is used will get updated as well. The only object that doesn't change its appearance is the one that you are linked to.

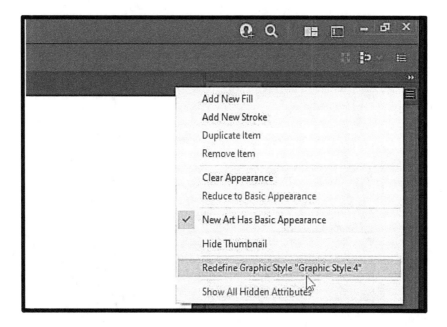

Now in some cases, you might want to keep both the original graphics style and the updated one - this is where the Duplicate graphic style command can come in handy. Drag the graphic style on top of the "New Graphic Style" button to easily duplicate it. You can then make the color changes and go again to redefine graphic style to update your graphic style. Moving to the next button, which is the trashcan icon; this can be used to remove selected graphic styles. Keep in mind that you can hold down the CTRL key or the SHIFT key to select more than one graphic style and remove them at once using this button. Once saved, graphic styles can be easily shared between Illustrator documents. Using the flyout menu you can open some panels with built-in graphic styles which you can easily apply, you can save your graphic styles using the "Save Graphic Style" command or you can open some other sets of graphic styles. Again, you can easily apply any of these graphic styles, and now that you know what all these buttons do let's focus on the remaining commands from this flyout menu.

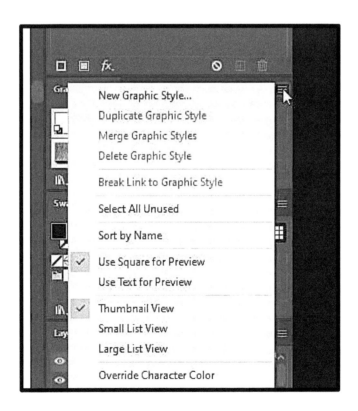

Starting with the Merge graphic styles command, let's say that you have two graphic styles that you wish to combine into a single graphic style, all you have to do is hold down the CTRL key to select both of these graphic styles, open the flyout menu and go to Merge graphic styles. Give this new graphic style a name; click OK to add it inside the Graphics Styles panel and now you can easily apply it. Next, you have the "Select all unused" command. This feature can be pretty useful whenever you wish to quickly clean up the Graphics Styles panel as it selects all of the unused graphic styles which you can then delete using the Delete button. Select "sort by name" from this drop-down menu whenever you wish to reorganize your graphics styles based on their names.

You can easily rename a graphic style as long as you have it selected. Just go to Graphics Styles options, type in your new name, and remember to click OK or press ENTER to apply the changes. You can check one of these two options (Live Square for Preview or Use Text for Preview) to preview your graphic styles either applied on text or a shape and besides this default thumbnail view, you have another two view options which can be pretty useful if you wish to always see the name of your graphic style using one of these List view modes. Keep in mind that you can right-click on any of your Graphics Styles for a larger preview. Finally, the "Override Character Color" feature will only affect the text from your design. Keep it enabled if you wish to remove the current text color as you apply a graphic style and if you disable this feature the graphic style will be applied to your text without removing the text color.

CC Libraries

One of the best things about Creative Cloud is the CC Libraries panel. It is extremely useful in all CC applications but in this section, we will take a close look at its role in Adobe Illustrator. Since the introduction of Creative Cloud libraries, Photoshop, Illustrator,

InDesign, and other Adobe applications have become better connected than ever before. In this section, we are going to give you a brief introduction about how it works and if you are a Creative Cloud subscriber this is something you must try out yourself.

How it works

The panel that you need is under the Window menu and it's called Libraries. Open that up and you can create as many libraries as you want; normally it would be a library either for a project or a client or even a type of work that you do and these libraries would be accessible from all the other Adobe applications as well.

How to save an asset in a Creative Cloud library

If you select any of your illustrations, all you have to do is simply drag and drop it and when you let go it will be added as a graphic after which you can easily rename it. You can select another one and again drag and drop it in and now it's saved.

If you select a text object it is best to decide how you want to import this by choosing "Add content" and checking the attribute that you wish to save so it can be saved as a graphic style or just simply the color that you used on it.

Let's try that. First, turn off the rest and choose "Add." As you can see, it will show up as a color but then if you choose the graphic option it will be saved as an outline artwork. Once again, if you go back and choose Character style this time then it will be saved as a style which means that you can easily apply it to any text that you have in Adobe applications which includes not only Illustrator but also InDesign and Photoshop.

Working with the Library

Just to show you how quickly you can reuse any of these elements, switch to an empty document then bring one of your graphics by dragging and dropping it. You can scale it since it's completely vector-based but you might notice that it says it's a linked file and that is because it is connected to your Creative Cloud library. This means you can edit this by choosing Edit Original but then that also means it will be updated on all your projects wherever it was used since you added this to your Creative Cloud library.

If you change the wording here then save this and go up to File > Save, this will update in the library as well and if you come back to your actual empty project it shows up there but not only there this time, it will also update in the other document. Using Creative Cloud library assets is very similar to working with symbols but they are even more advanced than symbols because they can be used in different Adobe applications at the same time and they will update in all of them at once when you edit and make a change on the original asset. Another thing you can use the Libraries panel for is to search on the Adobe stock website. Let's say you're looking for a tent, you're just going to type that here and this is going to search for images but you can look for illustration specifically or you can even choose vectors as the filtering option.

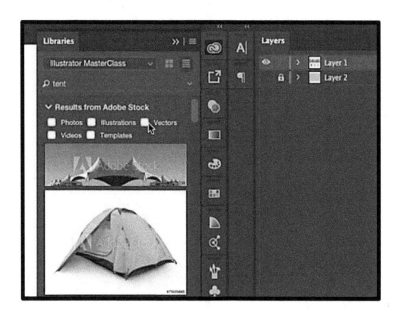

The cool thing is that if you find something that you like, you can add this to your library. You can save this and it will show up as a graphic here and you can even drag and drop it into your project. The issue here is that because it's not a licensed asset it's going to have a watermark on it but then it's still good to preview and check whether it's going to work with the style that you're working on and if your creative director or the client approves it then you can buy the license for it which would be as simple as right-clicking on it and choosing "License image."

Share and collaborate

If you want to build up a library that you would like to make public and make it accessible to other Creative Cloud users you can do that from the panel menu by choosing "Share link."

Once you click on this it will open up a browser window where you can turn the private option on to public which will immediately generate a link you can also decide whether you want to allow people to follow which means that they can see but not download your assets. If you allow "save as" then that means they can save copies of your assets into their projects.

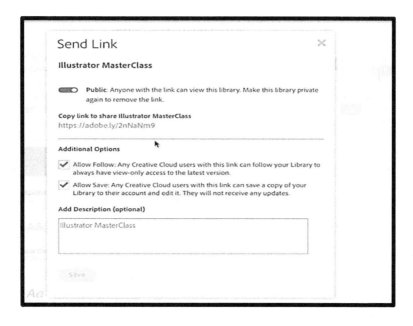

Similar to sharing your library you can invite creatives who are also Creative Cloud subscribers to collaborate and add their assets into the same Creative Cloud library. The way you do that from the browser is by clicking on the plus sign which will invite the collaborators. You just have to add their email address and decide whether they can edit or just view the library and while you are in the browser and going through your account you can also check all the libraries that you created, make changes to them, or even delete them. That's only something you can do from the browser.

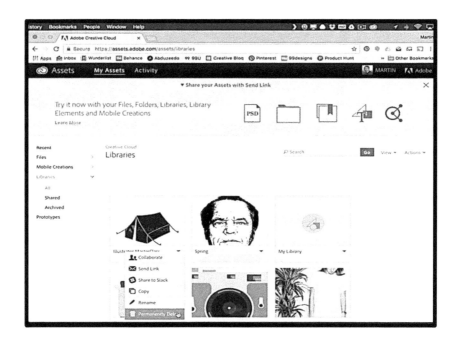

You can also find your mobile creations here which will display the different things that you've done in the Adobe mobile apps if you haven't started using Creative Cloud libraries yet we highly recommend giving them a go because they can streamline your creative workflow.

Review Questions

1. How can professional graphic designers use graphic styles in Adobe Illustrator to make their designs even better?

2. Give 5 tips for working faster and better with Adobe Illustrator as a professional graphic designer.

3. How do you save your assets in Adobe CC?

CHAPTER 15

DESIGN A T-SHIRT TEMPLATE

In this chapter, we are going to show you a quick way to design a T-shirt template using Adobe Illustrator.

Get started

A 14 X 18 document is what you start with, and then you insert your photo. What we need to do is cut out the background and a way that we do this is to take the Pen tool then go around the shirt and put a transparency mask on it.

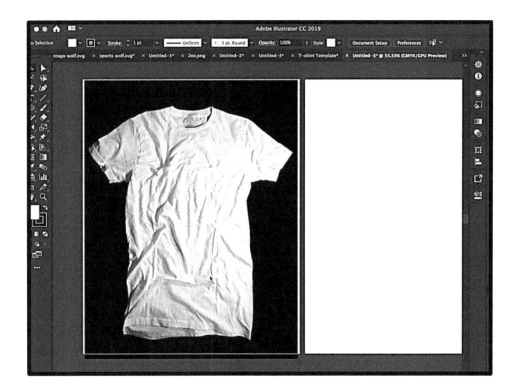

Applying strokes and fill

Now that we've got this shape we just need to go ahead and flip the strokes to fill and go into our Layers panel. We are going to copy that layer and then lock that layer down. This layer is very important.

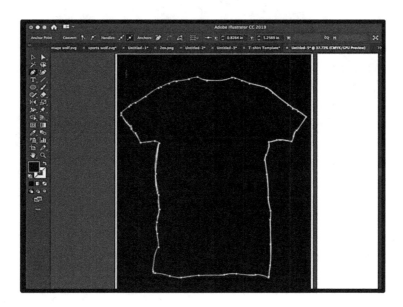

Applying transparency

Now we will go into our Shirt file and hit the transparency icon right here. If you don't see that you have to go into Window, down to Transparency, and click that. It will create that transparency icon for you. Also, make sure that you turn off the icons for the path that you just made.

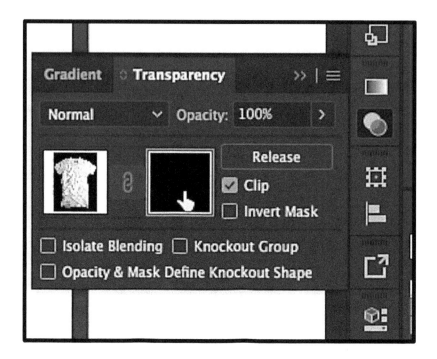

In this transparency, we want to go ahead and make a mask that should take everything out of the game. If we click on that mask or that black spot and we hit CTRL/COMMAND+F we'll paste in that shape that we just created. If we invert the mask we'll get the t-shirt cut out of the background.

Going deeper using the layers panel

We've just told you how to cut things out of the background in Illustrator. Now if we click back on this picture it'll bring back our Layers panel. A lot of times, people want to make sure that this is cut so they don't want to worry about the transparency and that's not a bad idea if you're like that what you want to do is to go to an object and rasterize and in this Rasterize icon make sure that you hit "transparent" for the background and hit OK. Doing that gets rid of the transparency mask and if used to move the t-shirt outside of the box you will see that the background is gone permanently.

Now we're going to take the image we want to rename it (we are going to name it T-shirt) and then make a copy of it. We'll click and hold this layer and bring it down to the "New" icon at the bottom just to make a duplicate copy and we are going to bring this copy above the path that we created. Now of course we don't have clipping masks which means that anything that we make will affect everything under it but because this t-shirt is cut up to a shape nothing behind this will be disturbed if we put something behind it.

What we are saying is when we put this t-shirt on a multiply effect layer in the transparencies, of course, the t-shirt gets darker because it's affecting the actual t-shirt layer. We don't have this icon here but if we were to unlike the path and turn on this icon is only affecting the black layer so if we change the color of this black layer to red, we have just changed the color of the shirt and this looks pretty good. What we are going to do is name this layer and lock that layer down for a second. Now we want to go into Layer Two and we're going to use the other side of the artboard to start doing some art. What we want to do is to paste in some art quickly and then put a black background behind it as well so we can see what's going on.

We can also change the color of the shirt to black as well so we are just going to copy this layer quickly, go ahead and lock that down then go into our t-shirt template and just make a new layer above that. We can just go ahead and hit CTRL/COMMAND+F and paste that in. Now we have our t-shirt template.

Review Questions

1. Explain how you can make a t-shirt template using Adobe Illustrator.

2. Explain the use of the Layers panel in organizing your work.

3. How can you add your graphics to a template in Adobe Illustrator?

CHAPTER 16

WORKING WITH IMAGES

In this chapter, we'll be sharing with you how to import an image to Adobe Illustrator. If this is your first time using Adobe Illustrator and you don't know how to go about importing images and locking an image so that if you're working on that image it won't be moving around on the canvas, this chapter is dedicated to showing you basic steps on how to import your image.

How to insert image in Adobe Illustrator

Adobe Illustrator is not like any other software that has an Import option as some basic software does. In Adobe Illustrator what we have is "Place." so we can use "Place" as our Import function. As you can see we have Export and under that, we have Export, Export to Screen, and Export As.

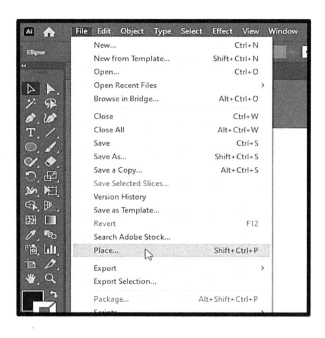

To import an image to Adobe Illustrator for the first time, head to the File menu at the top then scroll down and click on "Place." The shortcut for place is SHIFT+CTRL+P. Now if you click on that, it will take you to your folder where you have the list of all the work you have. There are different ways in which you can import an image to Adobe Illustrator. You can import it as a template link if you want to use it to replace the existing one and if you want to show Imports options so in the case of this chapter, we'll be sharing with you the easiest way. Click on the image you want to use, then click on "Place" and you'll see your image. Now it is left for you to place it on your workplace by clicking once and dropping it there. If you want to increase the size, rotate your image, or make it uniform, use ALT+SHIFT then you now increase or reduce it so that the shape will not deform because if you click on it now you might discover that it will deform. Also, if you want to place an image on your canvas make sure that it is centralized. If you move it closely you would realize that you see a center line there so ensure it is centered in your X and Y axis.

Embedding Images

This section will show you how to embed all images in Illustrator. First, go to the Window menu, go to Links, hold down the SHIFT key, and select the images from the dialogue box.

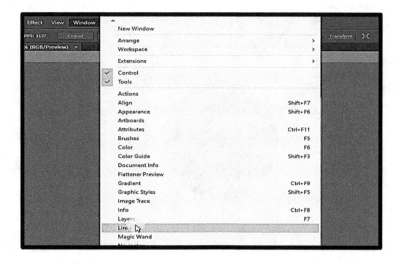

Then click on the menu icon at the top right corner and click on "Embed image."

Inserting an Image into a Shape

In this section, we'll be showing you how to insert an image into a shape in Adobe Illustrator. The first thing you want to do is to create the shape that you want to insert an image of so go over to the toolbar on the left side of your screen, Select the Shape Tool, and choose a shape. You can get these different shapes by right-clicking on the Shape icon right here and this displays all of the different options. For this illustration, select the Ellipse Tool then hold down SHIFT and ALT to create a circle. You can scale this up and give this color.

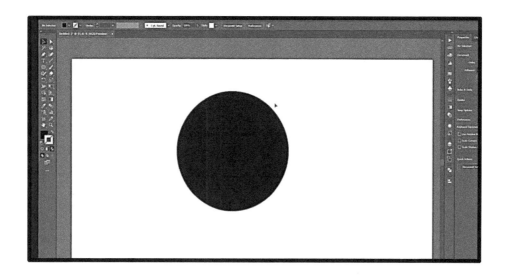

Now you're ready to insert the image into the shape. Press on the shape and the Toolbar goes down to the icon that says "Draw inside." The keyboard shortcut for that is SHIFT+D.

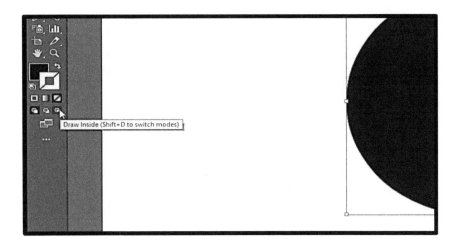

A border will appear around the circle and that's just fine. Now you want to press on the circle again then go up to File, down to Place (the keyboard shortcut for this is SHIFT+CTRL+P, then find the image that you have saved that you want to place into this shape so just select the image and press "Place."

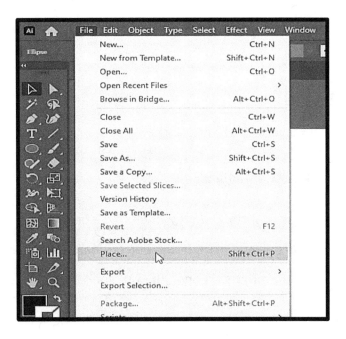

From here you want to drag around the shape and place it somewhere. When you have placed your image in this shape you can now just double-click on the artboard and you have now inserted an image in a shape.

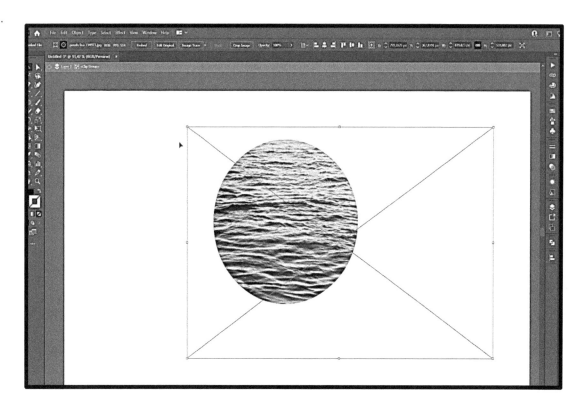

If you would like to change the image in this shape you can also double-click and change the position of this shape. This works with any shape you would like to use. You can also create shapes with the Pen Tool and this will still work.

Embedding Linked Images

In this section, we're going to show you how to embed a linked image here in Illustrator. Get your image then go ahead and place it on your Artboard as a linked image. With that image selected, go to the Properties panel, (if you don't see it it's going to be in the

Window menu), at the very top you can see it is a linked file (it says that right here). Now

if you click on this linked file you'll also see a little link icon indicator.

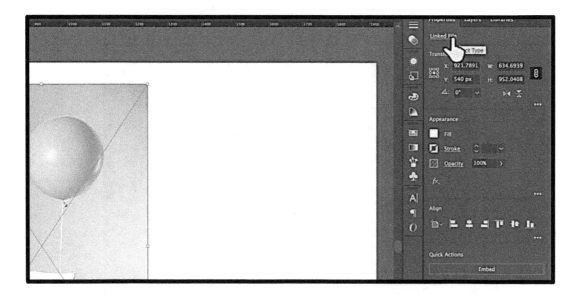

You can use this drop-down arrow right here to show more information about the link like

the location of the file as well as the resolution and dimensions and some other details.

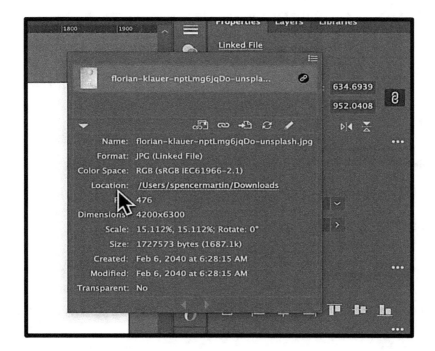

If you want to embed this image you would go up here to the hamburger menu drop-down from there. You'd see an embed image option.

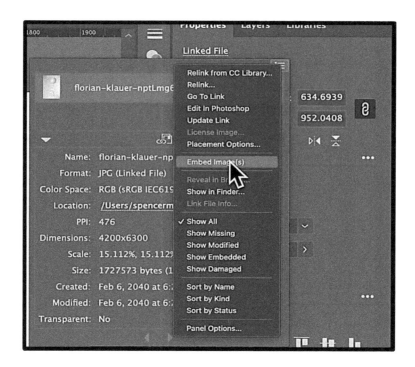

One important note here is: that this linked file needs to exist on your computer or your storage so it can't be a missing link or else it can't embed the image, however, if you have this image linked properly you can click this embed image option and it will remove the link property of that image and will embed it into your file. One other thing to note here is your file will increase by the size of that image because the image is now contained within the file so in this case, 1.6 megabytes is about how much bigger this illustrator file will be when you save it down. This matters a lot when you start to embed a lot of imagery into your Illustrator documents.

Review Questions

1. How can you add images to Adobe Illustrator to make your artwork better?

2. Explain how to make images bigger or smaller in Adobe Illustrator without losing quality.

3. What tools in Adobe Illustrator can you use to edit and improve your images?

CHAPTER 17

MASKING IN ADOBE ILLUSTRATOR

In this chapter, we're going to talk about a bunch of different types of masks here in Adobe Illustrator.

Clipping Mask

With this, you can simply use a shape to instantly contain your artwork within a specific area. This means you create the shape that you want to put your artwork within and that shape is going to be the mask.

How to Create Clipping Mask

Begin by creating a fresh canvas. You can make any size you like by altering the height and width in the document window, then going to the Tools panel and choosing the Ellipse Tool. Move to the top and select a fill or color. Hold ALT and SHIFT to draw a precise form, then center it on the canvas by clicking the Alignment buttons.

Next, import the photo by going to File > Place, selecting the photo, and pressing ENTER. To release the photo, click on the canvas, then hold down the SHIFT and ALT keys simultaneously to resize it from a single anchor point. Drag and drop it onto the shape, then use ALT and SHIFT to proportionally resize the photo. Right-click on the photo and send it behind the shape. To select all, use CTRL + A. You can also drag it to get the same result. Go to Object > Clipping Mask > Make. Even better, you may utilize the CTRL+7 shortcut to accomplish the same task.

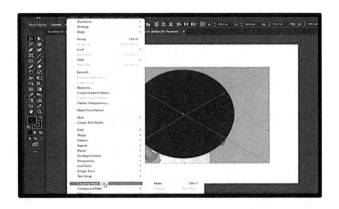

Now, if you want to alter the photo and drag it, but you notice it moves with the shape, which you don't want, hit Ctrl+Z to undo the action, then go to Object > Clipping Mask > Edit Content. Select the photo and place it as desired; hold ALT and SHIFT to resize it accordingly. It cuts out the shape while resizing the photo.

Go to the Layers panel and open the group accordingly. Select the photo right-click on it and choose "Isolated Clipping Mask." Hold Alt and SHIFT again and then resize the photo. Finally, click on the arrow to close the Layers panel.

Editing your Clipping Mask

When you choose your Clipping Mask, an icon called the Clip Group will appear in the upper-left corner of the Illustrator window, with two icons next to it allowing you to alter either the clipping path or the contents.

When you click the Contents button with that image chosen, you can rearrange it within the clipping mask. You need a way to get to the various components of this clip group because if you pick the entire clip group like any other group in Illustrator, the bounding box modifications apply to everything, and you risk accidentally squeezing your photograph. To edit a clipping mask, you can use the buttons on the top control bar or treat it like any other group in Illustrator, switching between your Selection Tool and Direct Selection Tool. For example, you can deselect the "Clip Group" and then grab your white arrow by tapping A on your keyboard then you can select the photograph inside, and move it around inside of the clipping shape.

If you want to select the shape, click on its edge with your white arrow and then switch to your black arrow. You can now edit the shape without disturbing the photograph, so whether you use the buttons on the top control bar or your Selection Tools, you can choose which part of the clipping mask to edit. It's also useful to examine clip groups in the Layers panel. Layer 1 is present in the Layers panel. If we expand this layer, we will see the clip group. If we expand that again, inside that we have the rectangle; that's our clipping path and the linked file is our image.

We may simply deselect here by clicking on the artboard and then independently choose either the image or the rectangle, providing another method for selecting the different components of this clip group. Also, while we have this form chosen, there is an underlining underneath it, indicating that this is the clipping path. Now that we have it selected, we can make more edits as we did before, but we also want to point out that there is no fill or stroke at the bottom of the Tool panel, which is what happens when you create a path or shape and use it as a mask; once you do that, that shape becomes invisible with no fill or stroke appearance, and this remains the case even if we release this clipping mask. If we go back to the Object menu, pick Clipping Mask, and then choose "Release," we will no longer have our Clip Group. When we check over on layer one, we see a rectangle with no fill and no stroke on top of the attached file.

That's how to make a Clipping Mask in Illustrator and knowing it from this perspective is going to help you when you get into more complex clip groups where you have lots of objects and nested groups.

Opacity Masks

In this section, we'll explain what Opacity Masks are in Adobe Illustrator and show you some fast examples of how to use them on your artwork. An opacity mask can be applied to any object you build, allowing you to specify the item's transparency with greater control. This will allow you to add visibility to your designs in unique and dynamic ways. For this illustration, we made a simple vector bird that we want to make more exciting by adding textures and gradients, which we will achieve using Opacity Masks. You can follow along using any illustration you have created in Adobe Illustrator.

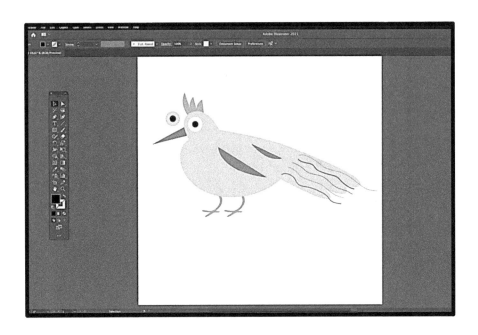

Before we begin, make sure you have opened the Transparency and Gradient panels, which can be located in the Windows menu. The Transparency panel houses the Opacity Masks. To demonstrate how this works, we will first create a shadow on the bird, then copy and paste the bird's peach-colored body into place before going to our fuel box and selecting a somewhat darker color than pink. With your object selected, you should see a thumbnail image to the left of the Transparency panel.

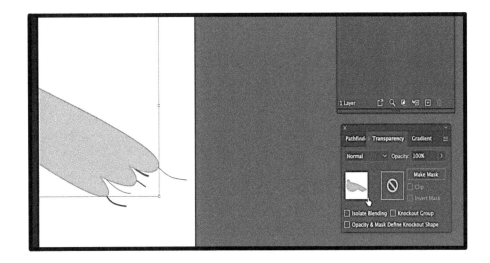

To create an Opacity Mask for this object double-click inside the empty box to the right, you will notice that your object has disappeared and the box is now black; this is Adobe Illustrator's default and it means that your object will have an opacity of 0%. In the Opacity Mask, the transparency values are represented as different shades of gray. Anything black in your Opacity Mask has an opacity of 0% and is invisible, while anything white in your Opacity Mask has an opacity of hundred percent and is visible. Any areas with different shades of gray will vary in transparency depending on their color.

We'll apply a grayscale gradient to this Opacity Mask. To accomplish this, navigate to the Gradient panel in the drop-down menu, select a grayscale gradient, and then create a vector object in the Opacity Mask. In this case, we'll draw a rectangle that covers the full bird's body, and we can see how our pink item fades out as its transparency values are dictated by the grayscale gradient. We've just added to the Opacity Mask, so if we go to the Opacity Mask thumbnail in our Transparency panel, we'll notice that it now contains the gradient we made.

Let's attempt another technique to use the Opacity Mask. To return to creating your illustration, exit the Opacity Mask by clicking once on the left thumbnail of the item. With this object chosen, we'll go to our Layers panel and simply slide it behind a few other objects to make the eyes and details on the bird pop out.

The next opacity mask we want to add is to the squiggly lines on the bird's tail. We want these lines to be contained to the bird's tail and not hanging out the ends. First, we are going to select all the lines and ensure that they are grouped as one object by right-clicking and selecting "Group." In the Transparency panel, we can now see the lines represented as one object in the thumbnail.

We'll return to our illustration, select the bird's body, copy and paste it, and then select white from the Field box. We'll copy the white object, erase it from our artboard, reselect the squiggly lines, and create an Opacity Mask by double-clicking the right box in the Transparency panel. Again, everything is set to black, and nothing is visible. We will paste the previously saved white object into place, and the lines will now be contained within the tail.

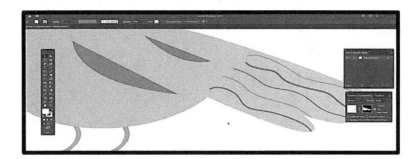

Review Questions

1. Why do we use masks in Adobe Illustrator?

2. Explain how to create a mask in Adobe Illustrator and use it to show or hide parts of our artwork.

3. What are some cool tricks you can do with masks in Adobe Illustrator, and how can you make them even more interesting by combining them with other tools?

CHAPTER 18

SAVING AND SHARING YOUR CREATIONS

Being able to share what you create with others is one of the reasons why we create. From sharing your art on social media with friends to sharing professional designs with coworkers, sharing your work for fun or collaboration has become more important than ever. Illustrator gives you lots of options for both saving and sharing your work in different formats for different purposes. We know you want to jump in and try this yourself, but let's first check out some examples of what we're talking about. Now, let's say you're making a graphic for social media, you set up your project and you start working. Unless you finish your project in one go, you're probably going to need to save your file so you can keep working later (we've all lost work because we forgot to hit Save). So Illustrator gives you a couple of different ways to make life easier.

Saving for the first time?

When you save for the first time by choosing "File," "Save" or you save a copy of a document, you can either save your work to your hard drive as an Illustrator file or online as a Cloud document. Whichever way you save, this will be your working dock where everything is preserved.

If you share it with someone, they can make edits too in Illustrator. When you save to your hard drive, it's like any file you save to your computer. You can attach it to an email or upload it to your preferred file-sharing service. But it only exists on your hard drive. So you'll need to create a backup manually.

Save to cloud

If you save your project as a Cloud document, it lives safely in Creative Cloud and is accessible from anywhere you log in. As a Cloud document, you can invite others to work on the file on their computers by sharing the file. Cloud docs automatically save your work for you. You can even see a version history in the Version History panel and roll back to earlier drafts if you need to.

Share for review

Once you're done with your project, you might want to share it with others for review, probably to get final approval. You can save your project as a PDF by choosing "File," or "Save as." Anyone can view the PDF even if they don't have Illustrator. They can use a free reader. Once approved, you're most likely to post the project on social media or website or anywhere else you need to post to a website or social media. You can either save the entire project or maybe just one part by choosing File, Export selection. You can save them as a JPEG, a PNG, or another format and upload them where you need them. To recap, you can save your file in Creative Cloud or locally, whatever is best for your situation. When you're ready to share your project or part of your project, you can do so in a format that makes sense like a JPEG or a PNG for social media or a PDF for printing or review.

Save the **Illustrator file as JPEG**.

A JPEG image does not include transparency just so you know; you're going to have a white background if you have any sort of transparency in your document. If you want to save your Illustrator file as a JPEG you can go up to the File menu, down to Export and you can do "Export for screens" or "Export as."

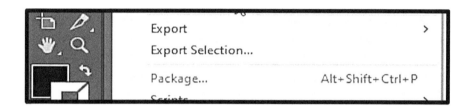

Export for screens gives you two tabs: your artboards or your assets. In the Asset Export panel, you can take objects in your design, right-click them, and add them here and you can export them individually.

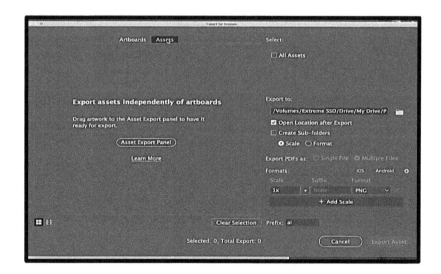

In the Artboards section, you're going to see all the artboards in your design and you can export them all at once or individually. On the right-hand side, you can see your selection of artboards. You can include the bleed or you can also export the full document (this means everything on and off your artboards) so if you choose this, it's going to export a JPEG of everything inside your Illustrator document.

You can then select where they save, whether you open it after export, you can create subfolders with different scales and formats and then you can select your formats down here. With this scaler here you can choose if you want 1x, like the size that it is in your document, or more. You can add a suffix and you can also change the file format. You can see other formats here but then JPEG 100 would be the best quality JPEG that you can export. You can add a prefix and then simply export your artboard. If you're creating thumbnails for something like a YouTube channel here in Illustrator you can export them as JPEG. To do that, go up to File down to Export and instead of Export for screens, choose "Export as." The "Export as" feature almost pulls up like the "Save" dialog box. Here, you can adjust the name but then when you want to select the format it might start on PNG so all you have to do is go down to JPEG. If you want to use Artboards you have to click "use artboards" or else this will export the full document like we showed before so click "use artboards," then select your artboard or a range of artboards or all and hit Export.

After you hit Export it's going to pull up some JPEG options. It's going to let you do different modes whether it's RGB or CMYK. You could even do grayscale, and select the quality (you can keep yours on 9 because thumbnails on YouTube are only two megabytes and 10 would give you a larger file than 2 megabytes) but you would use the maximum if you're trying to save the highest quality jpeg.

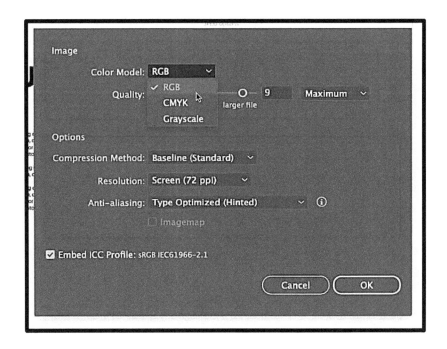

There are some compression modes here and the resolution, which is like the scale. If you have a 1920 x 1080 artboard and you export it at 72 pixels per inch that's going to export as 1920 x 1080. If you increase this, it's going to just double the size and almost triple the size on high or maybe even more. You can choose whether to export larger jpegs here and that's just going to increase the pixel count in the image. Now, remember, jpegs are raster files so they are going to be pixel-based, they will no longer be Vector but this is the way that you can export jpegs every day here in Illustrator.

Export Artboards as separate files

Let's say you have a project with four artboards and you want to export one artboard as a separate file, on the left side click on the Artboard Tool, click on the artboard and you can see the name of the artboard in the left corner. If you want to make some adjustments click on the artwork options in the Properties panel, click on Window, and check the Properties panel and you can change the name and size of the artboard. To save an artwork, go to File and "Save As" or "Save a copy." Let's say you want to save the second artboard, select a folder where you want to save it, and click on Save. Now in this window, check the box that says "Save each artboard to a separate file." If you do this, all artboards will save it as a separate file and you will have four illustrator files.

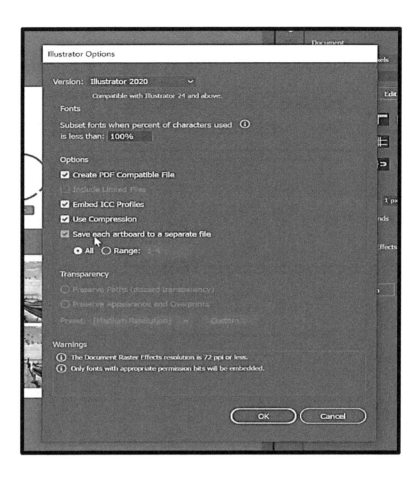

If you want to save just the second artboard click on the option that says "Range" and place 3 because you want to save the second artboard, then click on OK. Next, open the folder where you saved the second artboard and you can just rename it if you want and you have just the second artboard as a separate file.

Export with Transparency

Let's go over how you can export a graphic with a transparent background using Adobe Illustrator. To do that, make sure you have the object selected then right-click on it and go down to where it says "Export selection from" and the menu will pop up. In this menu, you'll see up here where it says Asset, go ahead and change the name of this to whatever you'd like your file name to be, and press ENTER.

If you come over here to where it says "Export to" you can click on the folder menu to choose where on your hard drive you'd like to save the file and then down here you can choose your file types. Here you only have one file type chosen but if you have other file types listed here just go ahead and click the X next to them to get rid of them since all you need is one copy and you need it to be in PNG format because PNG is the format that supports transparent backgrounds so make sure you have that enabled. Make sure you have the suffix set to none (if there's anything in there just erase it) and then over here where it says Scale, make sure you have this set to 1x. If you have this set to anything more than 1x it's going to export it at a different size than what it currently is and once you've done that you can go ahead and click on the "Export Asset" button and now your graphic should be exported as a graphic with the transparent background. If you open up your exported PNG graphic with Photoshop, for instance, and zoom in on this graphic you can see that this is indeed a transparent graphic as indicated by the checkerboard background going around the edges.

Review Questions

1. How would you save your work in different file formats in Adobe Illustrator, and what factors should you consider when choosing the right format?

2. Explain how to export your Illustrator artwork for printing and what are some tips to make sure the colors and files look good.

3. How can you share your Illustrator creations with others, and what should you be careful about to protect your work?

CHAPTER 19

ILLUSTRATOR SHORTCUTS YOU MUST KNOW

Illustrator offers an astonishing number of shortcuts, 233 to be exact. Fortunately, you don't need to know them all, but some are necessary, and in the long run, they can save you hours of labor. So we've chosen several that will benefit you. In this chapter, we'll explain why they're so crucial and teach you some strategies for using them.

Group/Ungroup

Groups are one of Illustrator's most important tools, and while you may assume they're only for organizing content, they can also be utilized to create certain visual effects. Some effects and features in Illustrator are applied differently to groups than individual objects. Strokes can be moved behind the items of a group in the Appearance Panel, resulting in a single outline for the entire group rather than one for each object. Similarly, effects such as Drop Shadow, Outer Glow, and Inner Glow behave differently in groups, influencing the entire group. Transparency can also be applied to the group as a whole, rather than individual objects inside it. Perhaps the most common reason we use groups is to position things on the artboard. Let's imagine we have some objects that we want to place in the center of the artboard. If we try to align them while they are ungrouped, they will just stack on top of each other; but, if we group them before aligning, the align function will consider the group as a single object, properly positioning the entire group in the middle of the artboard while without displacing any of the objects inside. Then we may simply ungroup them if necessary.

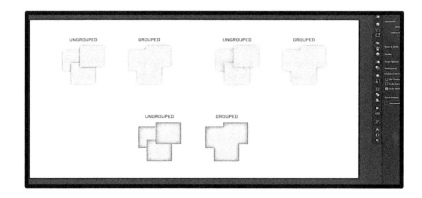

The shortcut for grouping objects is CTRL+G for Windows users, and CMD+G for Mac. For ungrouping, CTRL+SHIFT+G for Windows and CMD+SHIFT+G for Mac. The alternative way to group and ungroup is to either use the Object menu or the right-click menu.

Align

Since we're talking about object alignment, here's our next shortcut. Unfortunately, Illustrator does not have any alignment shortcuts. Fortunately, the align commands are available via the Object menu, which allows us to add custom shortcuts to them. And, while you can align using the Control Bar or the Align Panel, all of the icons are so similar that it always takes a few seconds to identify the one you need, and these seconds can add up to hours for a day. So let's make some new shortcuts. Go to the Edit menu and then select Keyboard Shortcuts. Change the Shortcuts window's shown shortcuts from Tools to Menu Commands. Then, go to Object > Align. Now you can add any key combination you wish.

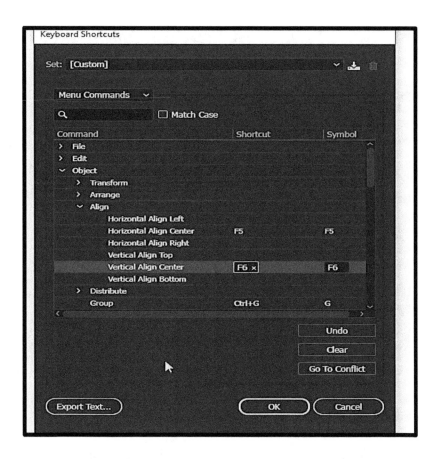

We like to use the F keys because they are normally tied to shortcuts in the Window menu, but we rarely use them, so that's alright. You don't have to provide shortcuts to every alignment choice, but at the very least include Horizontal and Vertical center. These are the ones you will use the most. Don't be scared to override an existing shortcut that you don't use; you can easily restore Illustrator's default shortcuts later if necessary. When you're ready, press OK, and Illustrator will urge you to save a shortcut preset; give it a name, and you're done. Now, whenever you have objects selected, you can just press the shortcuts you assigned and the magic will happen. After a few days of using this, you won't be able to go back ever again. But if you want to restore Illustrator's default shortcuts, just open the Shortcuts window and choose "Illustrator Defaults" from the drop-down menu.

Clipping Masks

Moving on, clipping masks are a vital element in any design workflow. If you're new to the term, a clipping mask is a technique for hiding areas of artwork using a specified form, which can range from as simple as a rectangle to unique, sophisticated designs. To construct a clipping mask, pick all of the objects you wish to clip as well as the shape that will serve as the mask itself. Illustrator will always utilize the object at the top of the stack as the mask. After you have everything selected, hit the shortcut CTRL+7 on Windows or CMD+7 on Mac to create the clipping mask and then you're done. If you want to release the clipping mask, you can use the shortcut CTRL+ALT+7 on Windows or CMD+OPTION+7 on Mac.

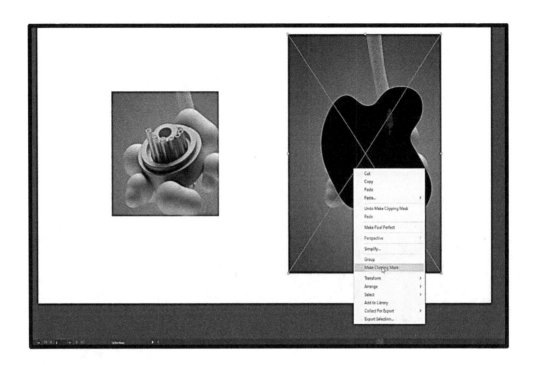

There is a great way to create clipping masks with text. To begin, outline the text by pressing CTRL+SHIFT+O (or CMD+SHIFT+O on a Mac). Then, use the CTRL+8 or CMD+8 shortcut on Mac to convert the text into a compound path. When you wish to construct a clipping mask with multiple objects, you'll need to use a compound path. Then simply continue with the clipping procedure as usual. Alternatively, you can create clipping masks using the Object menu or the right-click menu.

Arrange

To make it easier to adjust the stack order of your objects, utilize the Arrange commands effectively. In Illustrator, items are shown in a stacking sequence. If one object is higher in the Layers Panel than another, it will be higher on the Artboard as well. To modify the stack order, you have two options: drag the items up or down the stack using the Layers Panel, or use the Arrange commands.

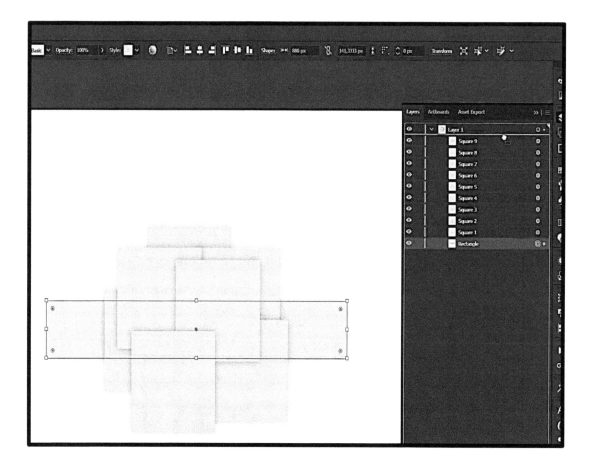

There are 4 of them: the first two are "Bring Forward" and "Send Backward." These will move the object up or down in the stack, one layer at a time. To do this, you can hold CTRL or CMD then use the close square bracket "]" to move up, and the open square bracket "["

to move down. The other 2 commands are "Bring to Front" and "Send to Back." These will send the object to the top or the bottom of the stack.

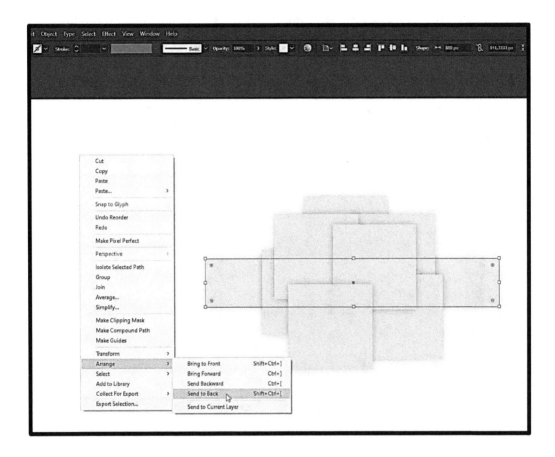

The shortcut is similar, but you must also hold SHIFT. So, CTRL or CMD+SHIFT+] (close square bracket) to bring the object to the top of the stack, and CTRL or CMD+SHIFT+[(open square bracket) to send the object to the bottom of the stack. The alternative way to access the Arrange commands is to use either the Object menu or the right-click menu.

Transform again

Working in Illustrator might be repetitive at times. Sometimes you have to generate multiples of the same item, or just duplicate something several times. We get it; it's boring.

This is where the "Transform Again" command comes in useful. This little-known command performs a very precise function: it repeats the previous change you applied to the specified object. This could include shifting, rotating, scaling, or duplicating. Let's see this in action. Suppose we want to move an object a few pixels to the side. When we use the Transform Again command, shortcut CTRL, or CMD+D, we observe that the action is repeated, and each time we use the command, it moves the same amount in the same direction. It works even when we choose a different object.

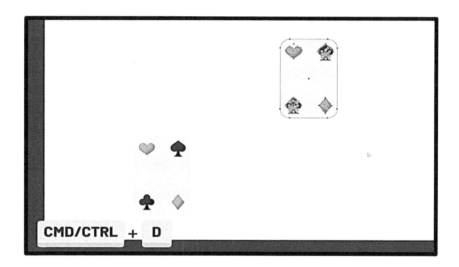

To make it more interesting, instead of just moving, we are going to hold the ALT or OPTION key while dragging the object. Holding ALT creates a duplicate of the object, and now if we use the Transform Again command, it repeats the entire action, creating a new duplicate every time, always in the same direction. Now we can select the entire row and repeat the process downwards. We drag the first time holding ALT and then press CTRL+D to repeat the action. Quite quickly, we've created a deck of cards. But what if we need to be more precise?

Let's try working with rotation. We are going to create a circle on the artboard using the Ellipse Tool, shortcut L, and then we are going to select the Rotate Tool, shortcut R, hold the ALT or OPTION key, and click once on top of the right anchor point of the circle. By holding ALT and clicking somewhere with the Rotate Tool, two things happen: we open the rotate window, so we can precisely input how much we want to rotate, but we also change the reference point of the rotation from the center of the object to the place where we clicked. Now, we can just input a rotation amount, let's say 20 degrees, and instead of clicking OK, we'll click on copy. This will create a new copy of the object, rotated 20 degrees around the reference point.

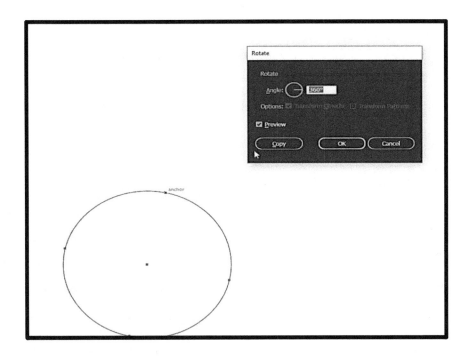

If we now select the copy and hit CTRL or CMD+D it will repeat this process of copy and rotation, and just like so we can easily create some very interesting shapes in Illustrator.

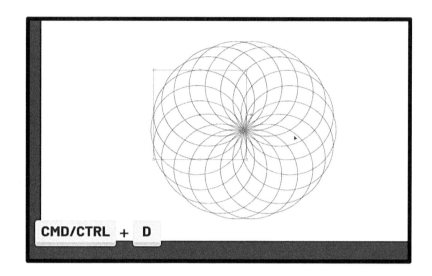

CMD/CTRL + D

The possibilities of this command are endless, but it might take some getting used to. The alternative way to access the Transform Again command is either through the Object menu or the right-click menu.

Trim view/Presentation mode

Sometimes things can get a little messy in our file, so it's great to have a quick way to preview the things we're creating without all these elements getting in the way. Thankfully, a few versions ago, Illustrator introduced Trim View and Presentation Mode, two amazing features to preview your work. The bad news: both of them don't have shortcuts. The good news: you already know how to create them. They're located under the View menu. Our keys of choice are F11 for Trim View and F12 for Presentation Mode, but you can choose whatever you want. Let's see how each one works.

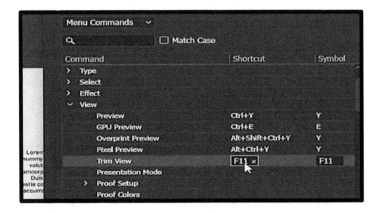

Trim View simply hides everything that is placed outside the artboard. Objects are still there, you can still select them, but they are hidden so you can have a better picture of how the artwork will look when it is exported.

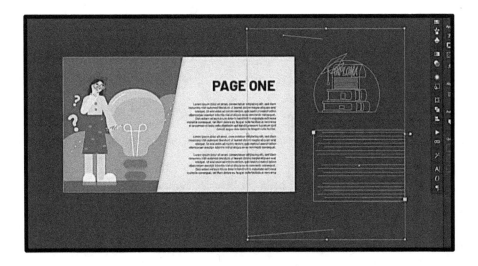

Presentation Mode, on the other hand, actually turns Illustrator into a PowerPoint of some sort. It will make Illustrator go full screen, with the artboard taking up most of the space, and hiding the user interface. It also prevents you from selecting anything in the artboard. Clicking anywhere or using the arrow keys will skip to the next artboard. One way we like to use Presentation Mode is when we are too lazy to export a design and send it for review.

We just press F12 to go to Presentation Mode, use Windows Capture Tool to take a Screenshot of the artboard, and then paste it on Discord or any other messaging app.

Expand/Expand Appearance

Expanding a vector object in Illustrator is just as useful as it is confusing, especially since we have two similar commands: Expand and Expand appearance. Let's understand what each one does once and for all. Both commands can be accessed through the Object menu, and in a general sense they do the same thing: they convert appearance attributes, which are literally what the name implies, into objects.

You can see an object's attributes through the Appearance panel - each layer on the panel is a different attribute. When you expand a shape, the attributes, like strokes, gradients, effects, or a blend will be converted to separate objects. The only difference between the two commands is that expand is used when the object only has basic attributes, like fill, stroke, and opacity. The Expand appearance is used when the object has other attributes applied to it, such as an envelope distortion, a drop shadow, or a distortion effect.

For example, let's apply a Twist effect on a rectangle. We can still edit the original rectangle and the Twist effect will adjust accordingly. This happens because the effect is applied as an attribute in the Appearance panel, and so the original shape is preserved. If we want to convert this effect into an object, or, effectively, apply this distortion to the rectangle, we can use the Expand Appearance command.

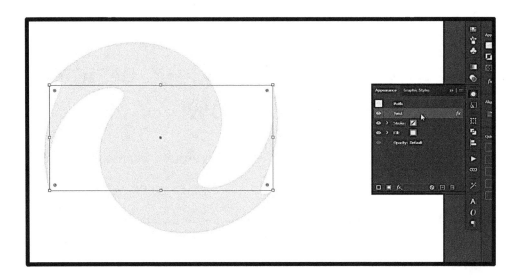

Now, the effect no longer shows up in the Appearance panel and we no longer have access to the original shape. It has been converted into its object, made out of paths and anchor points. We can do a similar thing with strokes. If you have an object that has a stroke, you can convert the stroke into a separate object by using the Expand command. Just select Stroke in the window that pops up and hit OK. Both of these commands don't have default shortcuts, so we have to create new ones again. Our shortcuts of choice for Expand and Expand appearance are CTRL+SHIFT+1 and CTRL+SHIFT+2, respectively. Replace CTRL for CMD if you're a Mac user, at this point we believe you got it already.

Review Questions

1. Why are shortcuts important in Adobe Illustrator?
2. List the shortcuts for arranging and grouping objects in Adobe Illustrator.
3. How can beginners remember and practice the most important shortcuts in Adobe Illustrator effectively?

CHAPTER 20

ILLUSTRATOR SECRETS GRAPHIC DESIGNERS MUST KNOW

In this chapter, you're going to learn 30 things in Adobe Illustrator that all graphic designers need to know and this bag of tricks will save you time, reduce frustration, and ultimately make your creative life so much easier.

Copy Appearance

To duplicate appearance effects from one object to another, select both, navigate to the Layers panel, choose the layer containing the effects you want to copy, hold **ALT or OPTION,** and drag one circle onto the other; all appearance effects are now copied across.

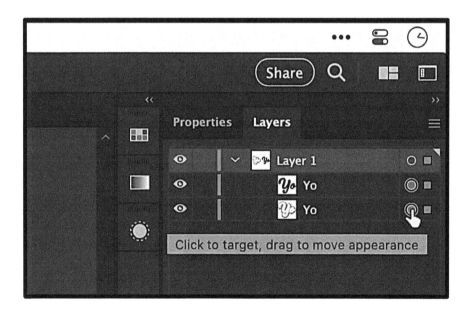

Easily create dotted lines.

Let's start by drawing a line, thickening the stroke weight. If we open the Stroke panel, we can tick the box for the dashed line, setting the dash to zero and the gap to whatever we like. Change the Gap type to round, and you'll get a dotted line. You can modify the distance by modifying the Gap value.

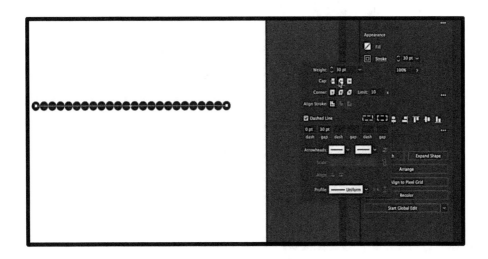

Intertwine two overlapping circles

If you have two overlapping circles, select them, go to the object menu, down to Intertwine, and click "Make," dismiss the helpful but rather unpleasant pop-up, and then drag over an area where the shapes connect to intertwine them both.

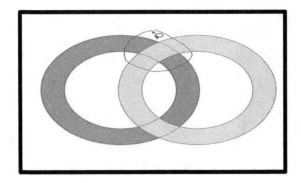

Get trimmed preview

If your artwork extends beyond the bounce of the artboard go to View and "**Trim view**" to get a trimmed preview.

Flip the direction of a curved line.

If you select the Arc Tool and click and drag to draw a curved line, while drawing the Line you can press F to flip the direction.

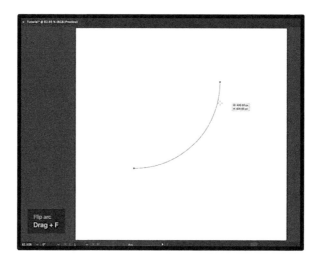

Clean up crooked curves.

Select the **Pencil Tool** and draw a squiggly line. As you can see, this is bad, but if you return to this menu and click and hold, you can select the Smooth Tool, and then click and drag repeatedly to go over the line to smooth out all of the curves. This is an excellent method for smoothing out any janky curves.

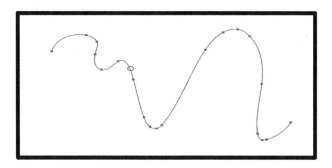

Switch to Smooth Tool

Following that, double-click the Pencil Tool and then select the option labeled "Option key toggles to Smooth Tool." When you draw a squiggly line, you can now use the shortcut ALT or OPTION to switch to the Smooth Tool.

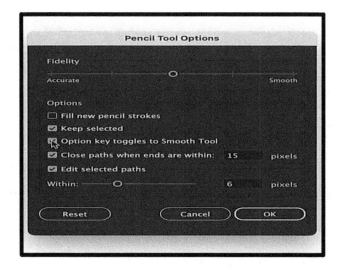

Cut straight line

We have a large red circle that we want to cut with the Knife Tool, so with this tool chosen, we'll click and drag while holding SHIFT, but it doesn't make straight lines. To cut straight lines, hold down ALT or OPTION while pressing SHIFT. Once you've made some clean cuts, you can divide the shape into individual pieces.

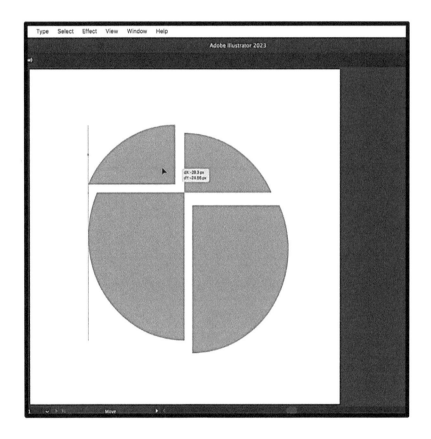

Highlight the end of a stroke.

Assume we have a gradient flowing from left to right. Let's select the shape and navigate to the Gradient panel. Make sure the stroke is chosen, and then click through the choices to adjust how the gradient is applied to the stroke. For example, if we select the middle one and then bring the slider's right edge in, we may put a highlight at the very end of that stroke.

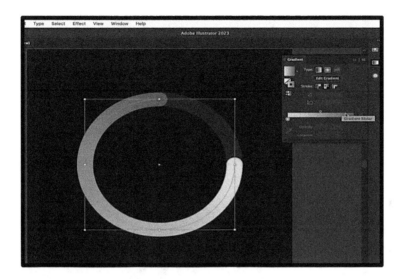

Reshape an existing shape.

Did you know you can use the Pencil Tool to reshape an existing shape? Let's imagine we have a large pink circle; we'll just draw some eyeballs, alter their color to white, duplicate them, and make them black.

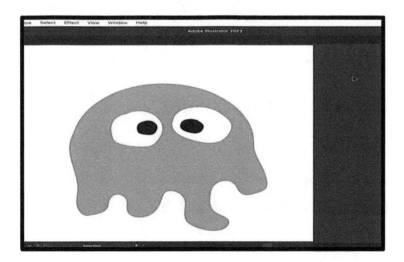

Get smoother curves

Here's another one with the Pencil Tool. Draw a terrible line and double-click the Pencil Tool. You can drag the slider to the right if you'd like smoother curves. Let's try that same curve again and you can see less accuracy but much smoother.

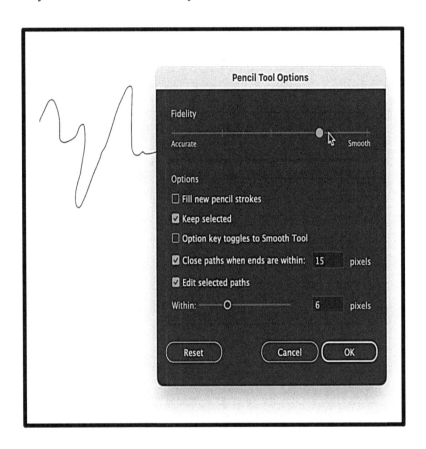

Use arrow keys to adjust a shape.

Next, we'll select the Star Tool, click and drag to create a star, and then use the up and down arrow keys to change the number of points. You may also modify the radius by holding down **COMMAND or CTRL and dragging.**

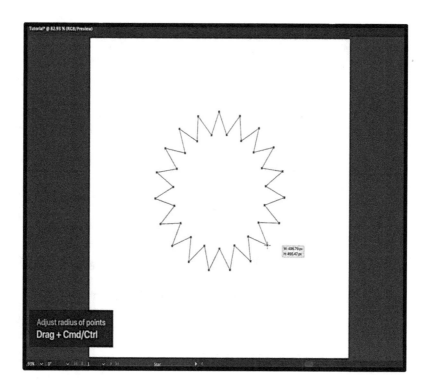

Move around using the spacebar.

Did you know the spacebar is a shortcut to use the Hand Tool to pan around? You can use COMMAND or CTRL plus or minus to zoom in or out. You can press Z for the Zoom Tool and COMMAND or CTRL+0 fits the artboard to the screen.

Using global swatches

We have some icons. If you scroll down in the Swatch panel, you can double-click one of the global swatches. Make sure the global option is checked, and if you activate Preview and modify the sliders, any changes to a global Swatch will be reflected throughout the text. This is quite beneficial.

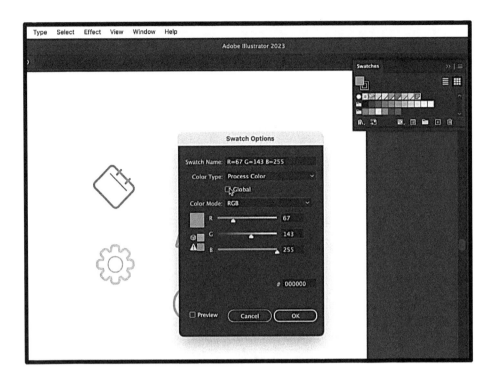

Applying tints

Now let's have a look at tints. First, navigate to Window and then to Color. Select one of these icons with a global Swatch, then switch to Color guide and set the base color. You can now click through the Tints to apply a tint to that same global Swatch, and the beautiful thing about this is that if you change the original color of the global Swatch, say red, all of the linked tints will be changed as well.

Editing a new document

How does one modify a new document? You can make a few changes under Document Setup, but you can also use the Artboard Tool to adjust the width and height of the artboard from the upper right corner. To alter the DPI, go to Effect and select Document Raster Effects Settings. From the drop-down menu, you may change the color mode or the DPI. You can also scroll to the bottom of the File menu to swap between CMYK and RGB color modes.

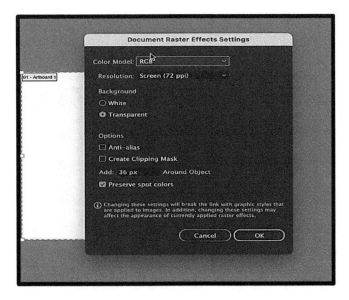

Rearrange Artboards

So we have an artboard with the Artboard Tool, let's add a few more artboards. If you encounter any issues, you can fix this mess by rearranging everything, choosing the layout type, you can adjust the number of columns, setting the spacing between artboards and that's it.

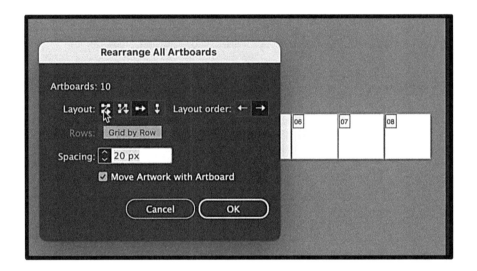

Get a wireframe preview.

- Go to View down to Outline to get a wireframe preview of your design.

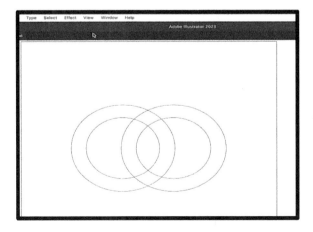

Combining shapes

Following that, pick the Shape Builder Tool, ensure the design is selected, and then click and drag between the parts to join them. This is similar to the new interweave function, except it is more permanent, and you may delete parts by holding down **ALT or OPTION when clicking.**

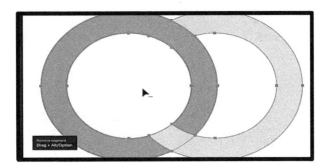

Cut a shape

Let's say you've got a blue circle. To cut, select the Scissor Tool and click anywhere in the circle. You may now use the Direct Selection Tool to choose a segment and remove it, and it will end where you cut. Remove any duplicate anchor points, and then grab the final anchor point and wave it about.

Sample exact color with Eyedropper Tool

Next, you can use the Eyedropper Tool to copy some of the properties from one shape to another but if you'd like to sample the color (not the shape properties), hold SHIFT and click and it will sample that exact color.

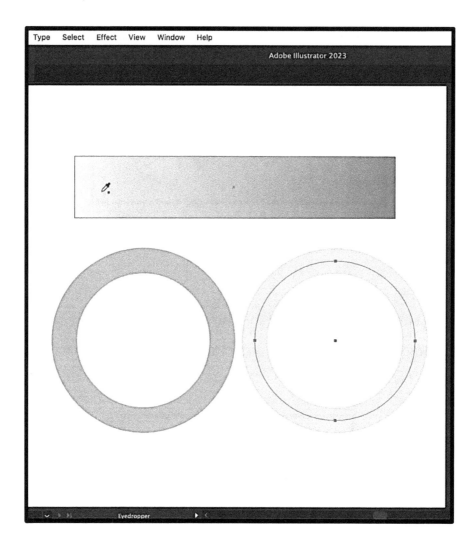

Advanced Eyedropper Tool Settings

Another quick tip: you can double-click the Eyedropper Tool and choose exactly what this tool picks up and applies.

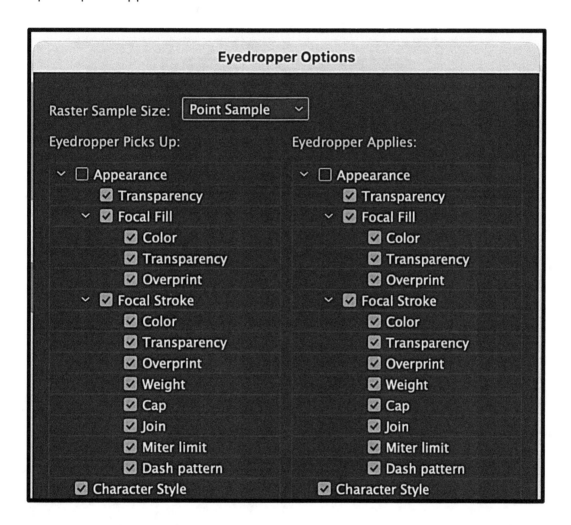

Working with arrow keys

You may be aware that you can alter an object's properties from the Transform panel using the arrow keys, but did you also know that you can hold down SHIFT to move in bigger increments or COMMAND/CTRL to move in smaller increments?

Adjust the **width and height of an object**.

We can also utilize the Properties panel to change the width and height of an object using math. We'll simply go to the end, minus fifty percent, and push return to make the circle 50% smaller. This also applies to addition, multiplication, and division.

Hide grid

At some point, you'll unintentionally select the Perspective Tool. When you do this, something appears, and like a sensible person, you try to click the extra close; however, nothing happens, and you go into a rage. Once you've calmed down, go to View, then down to Perspective Grid, where you'll see the option to "Hide grid."

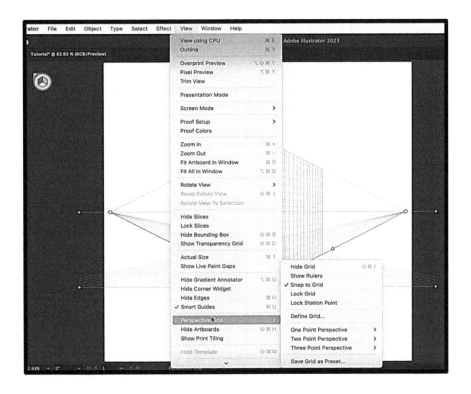

Double-clicking a group

Double-clicking a group is inception. You can keep double-clicking to go more layers in and a quick way out is to double-click anywhere on the workspace.

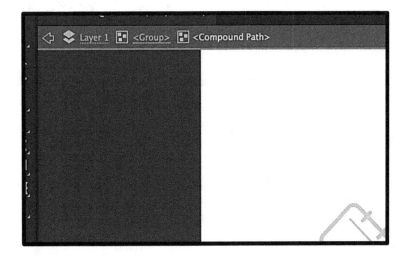

Brushes and lines

Another thing you may not be aware of is that you can go to Window, then down to Brushes, draw a line or shape or whatever, and then use the Menu icon in the top right corner to open the Open Brush Library and select from a variety of brushes that are compatible with Illustrator.

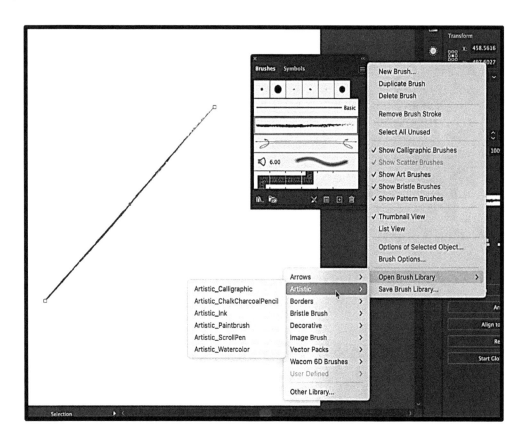

You can go for some paintbrush ones and with the line selected, you can click through and apply these different brush effects. You can also cycle through the brush categories from the bottom and you can also download and install more brush packs from other platforms.

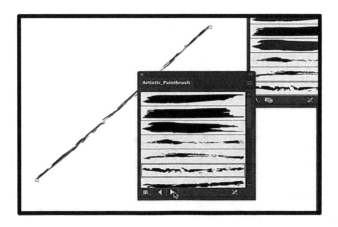

Separate intersecting shapes

We have some overlapping circles. Let's select them and select the "Divide" option from the Pathfinder panel and it will group these. So with them selected right-click and select "Ungroup" where all of these shapes are intersecting has now been separated into individual shapes and yes, this does look right.

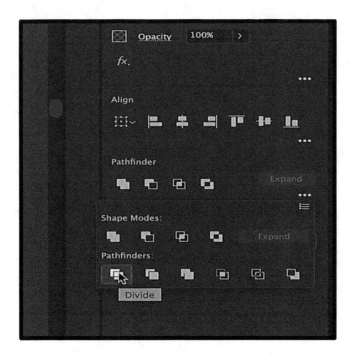

Go up to Illustrator's Preferences which is under the Edit menu if you're on Windows. Select Performance and increase "History States" to 200 so now when you screw up your design work you have the added peace of mind.

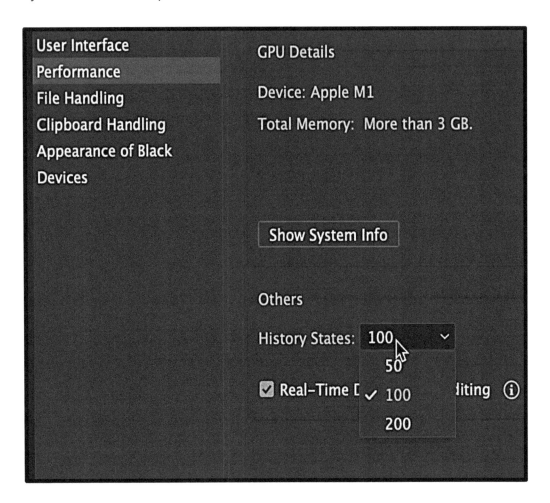

Change the **default location for saving files**.

Also, by default, Illustrator saves to the Cloud, but if you don't want to, you can go back to Preferences, click **"File handling**," and change the default location to prevent this window from appearing every time.

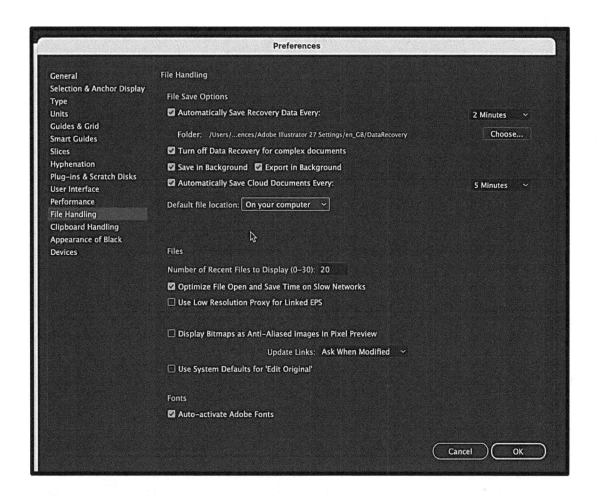

Review Questions

1. How can you intertwine overlapping shapes?

2. In what instance is a trimmed view important?

3. How can you copy appearance effects from one object to another?

INDEX

U

W

www.ingramcontent.com/pod-product-compliance
Lightning Source LLC
LaVergne TN
LVHW081517050326
832903LV00025B/1523